D1266545

9-8-66

A LISTING

OF THE WORKS OF

ROBERT NATHAN

WILL BE FOUND AT THE END

OF THIS VOLUME

Juliet in Mantua

Juliet
in Mantua

by
ROBERT NATHAN

~~~~~~~~~~~~~~~~~~~~~~~~~~~~~~~~

*Being the account of the
sojourn in Mantua
of Romeo and Juliet, and
their return to
Verona*

NEW YORK
ALFRED · A · KNOPF
1966

THIS IS A BORZOI BOOK
PUBLISHED BY ALFRED A. KNOPF, INC.

Library of Congress Catalog Card Number: 66–19985

FIRST EDITION

Manufactured in the United States of America

A NOTE TO THE PLAYERS

Juliet in Mantua is a comedy, and should be played for comedy, with merriment and with a certain sadness. I have kept the stage directions bare: "Enter, Exit, etc."; I prefer to leave the blocking, the polishing to the director. I should like him to put on the play as he sees it. Where I have been specific in my directions, I have followed the blocking of Ted Post who rehearsed many scenes with the actors and actresses of his workshop in Hollywood: as, for instance, his opening in which he has Romeo taking off his shoes and tiptoeing very carefully across the room to waken Juliet with a kiss—only to have her turn away, which lands him more or less on his nose. Or the scene at the picnic with the various comings and goings. It is actually the task—and the pleasure—of a director to bring his own enthusiasm to the play, and to stage it with as much imagination as he can.

As for the scenery, little more than a suggestion is needed, and a few props; the play is in the lines, not the scenery. The costumes can be of whatever period the director chooses; for myself, I favor the Byronic dress; as I say, what's time to Mantua? If one holds too close to period—to tights and ruffles and codpieces—the anachronisms (such as the feather boa) will appear awkward; the audience must be made to accept everything (after the first surprise) without complaint.

In other words: whatever group chooses to put this play upon the boards is urged to stage it freely, to experiment with it, and to have fun with it.

NOTES FOR THE DIRECTOR

JULIET is a lovely girl—and an unhappy one. She feels that "love" has let her down. She is both sweet-natured and spirited; capable of an almost childlike gaiety and innocence —and heart-deep feeling. The author is in love with her.

ROMEO is a frustrated romantic, self-centered, with an airy charm, humorous, wry—the boy who would like to grow up, but doesn't quite know how.

The NURSE is not a loud or explosive character. She is just a nurse, and should keep her voice down.

FRIAR LAURENCE has humor; he's a little sly, but in his way, wise. He can be caustic at times . . . but his heart is in the right place. He is patient with the world, from which he never expected much pleasure anyway.

LADY MONTAGUE is the mother of a son . . . which puts her one-up in the pecking order over LADY CAPULET, who has a daughter. LADY CAPULET knows this; she struggles, but she is not by nature a fighter.

PRINCE ESCALUS has a regal Elizabethan, or Welsh voice.

The PAPARAZZI are shrill and impudent.

PARIS is the suburban, Ivy-League husband . . . a little weary of his role, but not knowing any other . . . fond of his wife, but bored by her too at times . . . dreaming, occasionally of the moon-silvered past.

ROSALINE fits the part of such a wife . . . a bit fretful, bearing the burdens of the household—but with some hidden sweetness. A worried mother, but . . . also . . . a romantic girl; and when it comes right down to it, direct and breathless.

vi

Contents

ACT II

ACT III

Juliet in Mantua

Cast of Characters

~~~~~~

ROMEO MONTAGUE

JULIET CAPULET

LORD MONTAGUE

LADY MONTAGUE

LORD CAPULET

LADY CAPULET

COUNT PARIS (*The County Paris*)

ROSALINE, COUNTESS PARIS

FRIAR LAURENCE

NURSE

MESSENGERS

PRINCE ESCALUS AND COURTIERS, SOLDIERS, ETC.

REPORTERS ("PAPARAZZI")

A DRUNKEN MAN

ACT I

~~~~~~~~~~~~~~~~~~~~~~~~~~~~~~~~~~~~~~

SCENE I

[FRIAR LAURENCE *comes out on stage, and faces the audience*]

FRIAR LAURENCE: The place is Mantua, from the looks of it—some ten years after. The time:—but what is time to Mantua? The stones have weathered the centuries, and the palaces are only a little faded. People, like stones, last out the weather, and eat their sorrows with the same appetite one century or another.

Myself? I am that Friar Laurence that married Juliet to Romeo. It all began, if you remember, in Verona— Capulet and Montague at feud, one Guelph, the other Ghibelline; and Romeo, unable to get the fair Rosaline to bed with him, what between her virtue and his reputation, loses his heart overnight to Juliet, a Capulet —and must be wed to her in secret. It was a tangled story, the way it was writ; for Tybalt, Juliet's cousin, murdered Mercutio, Romeo's friend, whom, to avenge, our Romeo slew Tybalt, and was banished from the city. Meanwhile, lest Juliet be married to the County Paris, who was her parents' choice, I made some ar-

3

rangement for her to swallow down a sleeping draught
and so be thought dead. I sent post-haste to Romeo to
lift her from the tomb and carry her back to Mantua
with him. Alas, the messenger never left Verona!—and
hearing Juliet dead, as he supposed, Romeo sought a
poison from an apothecary, and rushing back to Verona
at night, stole to the tomb where Juliet lay sleeping
. . . a grisly tale!—as it was writ by our friend Will
Shakespeare, who got it from Arthur Brooke, who in
turn had it from Bandello—or perhaps Boisteau . . .
how a story grows from one kiss to another! Ah well!
Here's the honest truth of it; Bandello never knew that
the apothecary, mixing his poisons without prescription
and against the law, gave Romeo a simple powder
made up of alum and bicarbonate. So there he was
when Juliet awoke, with no more than a puckered
mouth. Not the first man to seek a hero's death, and
end up instead alive and married and headed out of
town. So here we are ten years later, in Mantua.
Romeo and Juliet wait out their banishment, along
with Juliet's old Nurse, and myself. That should be no
surprise! The Father General of our Order was glad
to get me out of the way of the authorities; and I myself felt responsible for the plight of these two sad
children, and therefore took upon my back, by way of
penance, the burden of their exile, and have kept them
company ever since, both as Confessor and man of
business, keeping account both of their hearts and of
their pocketbooks, these being the two things over
which lovers have the least control . . . that, and the
passage of time. . . .

[A MAN'S VOICE *is heard singing*]
> *A man going home*
> *In the dawn of the day*
> *To his wife . . .*
> *With the white lily moon on his shoulder. . . .*
> *What can he say? He's older.*
> *A short night older.*

FRIAR LAURENCE: Juliet is now twenty-four, and older than her years. Girls aged quickly in those days—and being married aged them quicker yet. Juliet was a woman at thirteen—or so we are told. "Her beauty hung upon the cheek of night like a rich jewel in an Ethiop's ear." So now it is dawn in Mantua; [ROMEO, *dressed in a long cloak, comes wearily down a narrow, mean street. He comes to a house with a balcony; he looks up at it as though he might attempt the climb*] night's candles have gone out. The man you see—it is a man—is Romeo, coming home, not unnaturally, to Juliet. I say home—but home is truly nothing more than a shabby house; one could rather call it lodgings. Ah well. . . . Let us listen now. "How silver-sweet sound lovers' tongues by night, like softest music to attending ears."

[A WOMAN'S VOICE *singing*]
> *A woman alone in her bed*
> *With the curlers and pins in her head*
> *In the dawn of the day*
> *With the buttercup sun on her shoulder—*
> *What can she say? That she's older.*
> *A long night older.*

[*During this song,* FRIAR LAURENCE *exits.* ROMEO *makes*

a half-hearted attempt to climb to the balcony, and then gives it up. It is obviously too much for him. Instead, with a shrug, he goes in at the door.]

SCENE II

[*In her bedroom,* JULIET, *in bed, turns ominously toward the door, as it opens.* ROMEO *is—how old was he when he left Verona?—still under thirty, but the look of youth has been worn thin on him. He is soberly dressed; his suit is frayed and mended; he wears a new cravat, and a rose in his buttonhole.*]

[ROMEO *comes in like any husband who has been out all night; and crosses hopefully—but not too hopefully— to* JULIET]

JULIET: Don't touch me!

ROMEO: But Juliet. . . !

JULIET [*Storming out of bed*]:   No, I tell you! And take your hands off me! I won't stand for it!

ROMEO: The dawn came up before I knew it.

JULIET: Then where were you, to let the night go by?

ROMEO: I was behind at cards . . . I couldn't leave. . . .

[*He takes a few coins from his pocket, and holds them out to her; she slaps his hand away*]

JULIET: I waited for you—all night long.

ROMEO: Darling—it's not that late! The nightingale sang me home.

6

JULIET: It was the lark, and not the nightingale.

ROMEO: Believe me, love, it was the nightingale.

JULIET: On the pomegranate tree? That sings so out of tune? It was the lark. You think this gray is not the morning light? Oh, fie!

ROMEO [*impatiently*]:   What shall I do, Juliet? I try to add to the few ducats my father sends me—the only way I know how. Is it my fault you get nothing from *your* family?

JULIET: Your fault! For being a Montague!

ROMEO: That was my parents' fault. Should they have sprinkled me a Capulet? At least, they remember me.

JULIET [*scornfully*]:   We live on cabbages. But never say my parents have forgot me! Only last year my mother sent me her love—and a feather boa!

ROMEO: It was an old one, and the moths flew out.

JULIET [*near tears*]:   It was her own—and all the clothes I've had, except for what I came away in.

ROMEO: And what your Nurse could pack. I came away in this, [*pointing to his jacket*] and that's ten years ago! You do not find that pitiful?

JULIET: It's pitiful to lie alone at night. And have no friends to visit with by day.

ROMEO: The night is made for sleeping, anyway.

JULIET: You said it differently ten years ago!

ROMEO [*glumly*]:   I did! I did! And I've learned better since.

JULIET: Sometimes I think I would be better dead.

ROMEO: God knows, I was ready to die! That wretched apothecary cheated me!

JULIET [*coldly*]:   At least—you can amuse yourself at cards.

ROMEO [*bitterly*]:   Amuse myself? For a few miserable
coins? God give me easement from such amusement!
Juliet—I'm weary to my bones!

JULIET: And what am I to do with wearied bones?

ROMEO: Knit them together, Madam!—or crochet!

JULIET: Thank you. That is not what I married for.

ROMEO: [*sleepily*]:   What *did* you marry for?

JULIET [*bitterly*]:   I have forgot. . . . To have a home,
I think. Or else for love.

[ROMEO *is asleep.* JULIET *wakes him*]

JULIET: Romeo!

ROMEO [*as though he hadn't heard the last part of the
remark*]:   You have a home.

JULIET: These—rooms a home?

ROMEO: I'll talk to you when you're more reasonable.
I'm going down to see if breakfast is ready. I've been
up all night. [*He turns to go*] Go back to bed, Julie.

JULIET: I have no proper bed!

[ROMEO *looks stupidly at the bed for a moment, and then
goes out.*]

JULIET:

    I said "or else for love."

               He did not hear.
His soul has clenched itself upon an egg,
And staggers cookward. And descending sleep
Falls like a morning fog around his head.
The voice that in my childhood lit my heart,
Yawns on its way to slumber. Alas, my girl,
Verona's far away, and childhood too;
As far as yesterday.

              The world's asleep,
And in the garden of my father's house,

The scent of jasmine mingles in the night
With flutes and fountains of the nightingales.
Lost, lost, a long time gone.
                  Ah, Romeo,
I said "or else for love."
                      God keep it so.
          CURTAIN

SCENE III

The main room of the lodgings, sparely furnished. FRIAR
LAURENCE *is seated before a small desk, writing with a
goose quill in a large ledger. He is doing his accounts;
there is a pile of bills on the desk in front of him to
which he refers; as he writes, adds, and subtracts, the tip
of his tongue thoughtfully explores the air outside his
mouth. He reads off his addition aloud.*

FRIAR LAURENCE: Four loaves of white ground bread
. . . seven sausages. Five cabbages . . . a small capon
. . . nine groschen, seven pennies. Four linen towels
from Genoa . . . seven sausages . . . again? . . . one
gentleman's cravat . . . seven florins! Hmmm! To
losses at piquet. . . . Hmmm! Four ducats in all. Four
from three leaves—what? Eh? Four from three!
[*He is speaking now to the* NURSE *who has come in,*

9

carrying a breakfast tray. She is quite old; ten years older, in fact, than she was when she left Verona. She comes to him, and looks over his shoulder.]

NURSE: You can't take four from three.

FRIAR LAURENCE: We do it, every week. We get three ducats from Verona, and spend four.

NURSE: Well, I'm sure it's not my fault, nor my mistress's either. Look at this old apron! I'm ashamed to be seen in it. It's enough to break a woman's heart. [*As she talks,* FRIAR LAURENCE *examines the breakfast tray; he lifts the cover from the pot of chocolate, and sniffs at it. He dips a finger into the honey.*] And her without a proper pair of hose these six months past. . . .

FRIAR LAURENCE: The chocolate smells good.

NURSE: . . . lying all morning in bed, her that used to be up with the sun, and her eyes grey with homesickness. . . .

FRIAR LAURENCE [*testing the chocolate*]:   A little too sweet, perhaps?

NURSE: . . . and what about myself? I have a nephew I haven't seen for ten long years; for all I know he's been in the army and out again, and is dead as a mackerel, or married; and not so much as a word from him all this time. And as for my Lord Romeo— Leave the toast alone. It's not for you.

FRIAR LAURENCE: She won't miss it, Nurse. She eats so lightly.

NURSE: And whose fault is that? She used to eat her porridge in the morning, two bowls of it, *and* strawberries and chocolate; and singing all day long. . . . [*Exasperated*] Now I shall have to toast another slice.

[*She starts back toward the kitchen;* ROMEO *entering from R. stops her*]

ROMEO [*with charm*]:   Stay, Nurse . . . take this flower to your mistress with my love. It still has dew upon it. [*He takes the flower from his buttonhole and hands it to the* NURSE, *who goes out.*] Commend me to her mercy. [*Seating himself wearily.*] Juliet is angry with me.

FRIAR LAURENCE: What else did you expect, my son? Night after night, out till all hours—gambling! Tsk!

ROMEO [*throwing a few coins on the table*]:   We have to live.

FRIAR LAURENCE: Of course. After all you've been through, it would be a shame not to. Still—two florins? Is that all? For a whole night's play at cards?

ROMEO: What else can I do? There's no other employment in Mantua for a foreigner. And our two families still at swords' points at home, and afraid to help us lest they be thought too forgiving. What's to forgive, but love? Juliet's parents have forgiven her to the extent of a feather boa. Mine—as you know.

FRIAR LAURENCE: Exile is a sad way to live, my son; and no one knows it better than myself. But sad or not— you do live. Give thanks for that.

ROMEO: I gave my thanks ten years ago. Like my clothes, they've worn thin. I have no joy in living, Father. I should be moldy bones.

FRIAR LAURENCE: Tst!

ROMEO: We were star-crossed lovers; it should have ended so. Life has double-crossed us.

FRIAR LAURENCE: Now that's a foolish way to talk! Marriage is a blessed state, my boy; and to achieve it one

has to put up with a certain amount of martyrdom. Still
—I confess—I thought the banishment would be eased
before this. I don't like Mantua any more than you do.
A dreary city. I miss my little cell in Verona—my own
herbs, my own plants— [*wretchedly*] I buy them at
the greengrocer's, and they're all out of rosemary.

ROMEO: Rosemary is for remembrance. They have forgotten us. . . . No, no! My family will send a message
yet to get us out of here! [*A little doubtfully*] Do you
think so, Father?

FRIAR LAURENCE: They'll have you home again, pray
God.

ROMEO: But God's in heaven—and heaven's in the sky
above Verona.

FRIAR LAURENCE: Which is the theologian—you or I?
God is everywhere; and heaven for you should be in
Juliet's bedchamber.

ROMEO: I wonder at you, Father!

FRIAR LAURENCE: Don't give me any pious looks, my
boy . . . I've known you too long; and the acquain-
tance has been in no wise edifying. Do you remember
when you could neither eat nor sleep, for mooning
after Rosaline? And then, in the twinkling of an eye,
you're up another balcony altogether. It was all I
could do to get the blessings of Holy Church into bed
with you, you were in such a hurry.

ROMEO: We were young, Father.

FRIAR LAURENCE: You were not too young to put your
sword through Tybalt.

ROMEO: I fought with Tybalt most unwillingly; if he
had been a Paduan, and we at war, I'd have had a
medal for it. The times are out of joint . . . but that's

from *Hamlet.* [*He yawns and rises.*] I'm going to the kitchen for an egg. Shall I have it poached . . . or fried . . . or dropped upon the floor?

FRIAR LAURENCE: Like yesterday. . . .

[NURSE *comes out of kitchen, at L. with the tray on her way to* JULIET's *room, crosses, and exits R.*]

ROMEO: I am a clumsy cook. Commend me to your patience, Father—and pray for a message from Verona. I sometimes think it is our only hope. We try, Father; we do try, the both of us. But we started large, and have come down too small.

[*He goes out.*]

CURTAIN

SCENE IV

[JULIET's *bedchamber. It is a simple room, barely furnished; a bed, a small sofa, a combination desk and dressing table, a chair. Her few clothes hang in a closet— including the pink feather boa sent to her by her mother. There are a few souvenirs of her childhood scattered about: a doll, dried flowers, seashells. Before the curtain rises—or the scene commences—a* WOMAN's VOICE *is heard singing:*]

Where do the young days go?
They go where the roses go

When summer is done.
And where does laughter go?
It goes where the young days go.
And Oh! The young lovers
Who promised each other that love was forever . . .
That never . . . that never . . .
Where have the young lovers gone?
Where does love go?

[*The* CURTAIN RISES *on* JULIET *alone. She stands a moment, as though listening; then she goes to the desk and opens a drawer from which she takes a box, and from it brings out a ribband; she tries it in her hair. She goes to the closet and takes out the feather boa and drapes it around her shoulders. She goes back to the box and takes out an old dance-card; it is the dance-card for the cotillion at which she met* ROMEO. *As she reads down the list of dances, she takes a few steps here and there—dreamily, but not very gaily. It is a rather forlorn evocation.*]

JULIET: Lancers . . . Cousin Manfredo. How are you, Cousin? And how is life in Rimini? Ah. Minuet. . . . No, Valentio, I'm afraid I'm promised . . . Polka . . . County Paris. [*She stands a moment, and makes a wry little face, half rueful, half-amused.*] Saraband . . . who was that with? I cannot read it . . . Quadrille . . . Lucio. [*She draws back with a grimace.*] Garlic! Waltz. . . Tyb. . . . [*She shakes her head.*] No. Poor Tybalt! [*She sighs deeply.*] Grand March . . . R.M.

[*She stands still, lost in a sad reverie, as* NURSE *enters.*]

NURSE: Commend me to her mercy, he says. And why would he say that, dearie? Have you been quarreling again?

JULIET: [quickly and defensively]:   No—certainly not!
It's only that he says things sometimes that he doesn't
mean. [*pitifully*] Does he?
[*She takes off her boa, gives it to* NURSE, *who hangs it in
the closet.*]

NURSE: Of course not, dearie! What did he say?

JULIET [*in a small voice*]:   He said he wished the
poison had killed him.

NURSE: Holy Saint Catherine! Did he say that?

JULIET: Perhaps I was at fault. . . .

NURSE: You were not! He was at fault for opening his
mouth. And that reminds me. . . . The water closet is
leaking again.

JULIET [*sitting on bed*]:   Oh dear! Not again! [*Pause*]
He said my family had forgotten me.

NURSE [*setting her back in the bed*]:   He did? Why, the
villain! I'm sure he's mistaken. There'll be a messenger
any day now from Verona, you'll see! Your father's
working on it.

JULIET: Do you know one of the last things my father
said to me? He said he had a curse in having me. He
called me Slut.

NURSE [*bringing the tray to* JULIET]:   I know. I was
there. . . . He would have married you to County
Paris.

JULIET: It would have been his own wedding, then—
not mine. He loved the Paris name. But I loved
Romeo—from the first moment I saw him. And when
he kissed me—

NURSE: It was too soon altogether—

JULIET: It was quite usual in my day, Nurse. He kissed
by the book. [*She starts to eat.*]

NURSE: I knew a wench married in an afternoon as she went to the garden for parsley to stuff a rabbit. That book was a history of the wars: a shrewd tale, but she was tamed by it.

JULIET: He looked at me—and he *saw* me; something opened, deep in his eyes . . . and he saw me. Most people don't see you, Nurse; they look at you, but they don't see you. He saw me. And then he kissed me.

NURSE: It was the most expensive look, then, in the known history of the world.

JULIET: Still—we do nicely, Nurse—do we not? For ones in modest circumstance?

NURSE: It would be nicer if you had some visitors to liven up your days.

JULIET: Oh—they will come. Besides—we're not here forever; someone will reach the prince, and call us home. [*Wistfully*] I would prefer it were my own family—

NURSE: [*warily*]: Still—it's a busy life, dearie, there at home—for Montagues *or* Capulets.

JULIET: Marriage is very different than I thought.

NURSE: It's too much for any woman—

JULIET: Do you think so? Sometimes I wonder. One can't keep shining like a constant moon . . . the nights are too long. If love goes out of the window—what then?

NURSE: You find it, Ma'am—and call it back again.

JULIET: I have no mother's rules to go by, Nurse. Not even a list of recipes. I learn as best I can, from the poets. They tell me that once married, people live happily ever after. Do you believe it?

NURSE: I was but married once, and I've lived ever after, but whether happily or not, I wouldn't know. . . .

JULIET: Perhaps if we were home. . . .

NURSE: Ah! Then you'd see the lilies blooming in your cheeks. . . .

JULIET: The roses, not the lilies.

NURSE: I know, I know, I get confused. . . .

JULIET: Truly, I think that Romeo does his best—within his nature. [*Looking at the rose*] "Commend me to her mercy." [*She twines the flower in her hair.*] How do I look?

NURSE [*fondly*]: You look like a mooning girl.

[ROMEO *enters; the* NURSE *takes up the tray and goes out. She indicates to* ROMEO *that all is well.*]

ROMEO [*uncomfortably*]: I thought I'd see if you were still awake. . . .

JULIET: My day has just begun. . . . Was I horrid to you?

ROMEO: A little. But I forgave you.

JULIET: Come here and talk to me a while.

[ROMEO *crosses hopefully to her; she makes conversation.*]

JULIET: What's the day like? Did you walk home?

[ROMEO *tries to reply, but she gives him no opportunity.*] I slept a little. You look tired. Are you tired, Romy? Did you get something to eat?

ROMEO: I dropped an. . . .

JULIET: You have a new cravat! Oh—it's very handsome!

ROMEO [*proudly*]: Pure silk. From Venice. It was a bargain.

JULIET [*Feels the cravat*]: Mmmmm! . . . Your coat

could stand a brushing. Get me my sewing basket and
I'll sew that button on for you. . . .

ROMEO [*surprised*]:   You will?

JULIET [*simply—but hopefully*]:   I was taught the cross-
stitch in school.

[ROMEO *goes to fetch the sewing box on the bureau; he
returns and, taking off his coat, hands it to* JULIET *and
follows her—rather uncertainly—to a small couch across
the room.*]

[JULIET *threads a needle, and sews the loose button on.
But* JULIET *does not sew very well. She had been brought
up like most of the girls her age—to stitch on samplers,
to dance the minuet, to speak French—a little—and to
play the lute . . . or possibly the mandolin. Not to sew
buttons on gentlemen's coats. She gives it her desperate,
awkward attention.*]

JULIET: How long have you had this coat, darling? You
really need a new one.

ROMEO: I know. . . . But. . . . [*He shrugs helplessly.*]
You could do with a new gown yourself.

JULIET: Things will be better some day. When we are
home again. Nurse has a cousin who is a dressmaker
near the Church of San Zeno Maggiore. Nurse says
she's very reasonable. I thought perhaps a sprigged
muslin, with a. . . .

[*pricking her finger with the needle*]
Oh! Oh dear!

[*She stares at it in dismay.*]

ROMEO [*sympathetically*]:   Mmm! Kiss it?

[*She holds out her finger and he kisses it.*]
Better?

JULIET: Much!

ROMEO: Do you know . . . I hate growing old, Julie.

JULIET: I know.

ROMEO: To feel—that I'm not—

[*He can't quite say it.*]

JULIET: Romantic? Any more?

ROMEO [*relieved*]: Yes. . . . Tell me—did we ever call your father Old Man Capulet?

JULIET: Certainly not.

ROMEO [*crossing stage; with a sad, wondering awe*]: They call me Old Man Montague. Young people have no—no feelings nowadays.

[ROMEO *begins to pat his stomach.*]

JULIET: They're very bold. I saw a young girl yesterday in the Square . . . a child, really; she couldn't have been more than fourteen. She wore a heavy beauty patch on her chin, and her hair was all done up in ringlets. Imagine!

ROMEO: I know. And the way they show their . . . [*catching* JULIET's *eye fixed on him; uncomfortably.*] Hmmmmm.

JULIET: Oh? . . . Darling—must you?

ROMEO: Must I what? You were fourteen when I met you.

JULIET: Thirteen. . . . Must you thump your stomach?

ROMEO: What else should I do with it?

JULIET: I wish you'd stop.

ROMEO: When a man has a stomach, he may as well thump it.

JULIET: You haven't *got* a stomach! [*Tentatively, she pats at her under-chin with the back of her hand.*] Is it a little plump? Here . . . put this on . . . [*She holds the coat out to him; he slips it on. She has sewed*

*the button in the wrong place. They both look help-
lessly at the result.*]

JULIET [*wretchedly*]:   I'll have Nurse do it.

ROMEO: It's beautifully stitched.

JULIET [*hopefully*]:   Is it really?

ROMEO [*not too sure*]:   I . . . think so . . .

[*They turn awkwardly away from each other.*]

ROMEO: Julie . . . if you had it to do . . . would you
do it all over again?

JULIET [*puzzled*]:   The coat?

ROMEO [*shaking his head*]:   Me.

JULIET [*slowly*]:   I still think you're the most attractive
man I've ever met.

ROMEO: I suppose that will have to do . . . I'm tired.

JULIET [*sitting down on the couch and holding out her
arms to him*]:   Rest awhile. . . .

ROMEO [*going to her*]:   Yes. . . .

JULIET [*begins to rock him*]:   There. . . .

ROMEO: I think my mother held me this way once. It
might have been an aunt. . . .

JULIET: Mmmm. . . .

[*She begins to hum, to sing quietly*]

      Lavender's blue, dilly dilly,
      Lavender's green.
      When you are King, dilly dilly,
      I shall be Queen.

ROMEO [*drowsily*]:   What's that, Julie?

JULIET [*lightly*]:   Oh . . . nothing. A child's song . . .
I used to sing to my dolls when I was young.

ROMEO [*yawning*]:   Your dolls?

JULIET [*lightly, but tenderly*]:   I always thought to have
a child; but not so solid a one.

ROMEO: Am I so heavy?

JULIET: Too light for a son—and too substantial for an ancestor. We ought to diet. . . . My Aunt Lavinia had a very good one. It seems you eat nothing but persimmons.

ROMEO: Persimmons? Good God! They set my teeth on edge! . . . I wish I had a son, Julie.

JULIET [*rising to downstage R.; this is a sore point with her*]: To be born in exile? In lodgings? In a borrowed room—in a borrowed land?

ROMEO: I wish you wouldn't keep saying that.

JULIET: What else should I say? It's true, isn't it?

ROMEO: I've tried to make you happy—

JULIET: Have I done any less? Do you think I like it here? Or that I'm never homesick. . . ? For my own. . . ?

ROMEO: I thought you loved me.

JULIET [*wearily*]: I do. I have nothing else to love.

ROMEO [*hurt*]: I see. Well—thank you, then, for nothing. [*He rises to downstage L.*]

JULIET [*going to him*]: I have nothing else but you to love! You're my whole world! That's all I mean! *Of course* I wish I had a child—a son, a daughter—anything! But not here! Not here! Can't you understand?

ROMEO [*hesitating*]: I guess so—

JULIET: It frightens me, to have so little. We cling together here in Mantua. . . . But if we ever went back into the world . . . what then? Would you still turn to me—or look for someone else to love? Do you think I never think of that? I hate to grow old . . . all alone . . . it haunts my nights!

ROMEO: You know I'll never leave you, Julie.

JULIET [*gently and sadly*]:   I hope not, my dear. It
would be marvelously sad otherwise. Never mind—I'm
always a little melancholy in the morning. I seem to
carry some shadow of the night into my waking. It
takes the sun to cure it; and a little exercise. Run
along, darling, get some sleep; and let me get dressed,
and do my marketing. . . .

ROMEO: Yes.

[*He bends to kiss her dutifully, and turns to go.*]

JULIET: And . . . Romeo . . .

ROMEO [*turning back*]:   Yes, Juliet?

JULIET: I love you.

ROMEO: I know. I love you, too.

[*He starts out again.*]

JULIET: Darling—

ROMEO: Yes?

JULIET: I . . . I have forgotten why I called you back.

ROMEO: Good night.

[JULIET *waves him a kiss as he goes out.*]

CURTAIN

[*A* MAN *and a* WOMAN *are heard singing*]:

MAN: *I had a father kind and true!*

WOMAN: (*He was a nasty martinet!*)
    I had a father just like you—

MAN: (*That one I'd just as soon forget!*)

WOMAN: *I had a lovely farthingale,*
    A cloak of gold, a gown of green. . . .

MAN: *I used to watch the stars grow pale,*
    And no one asked me where I'd been. . . .

WOMAN: *I danced a pretty saraband—*

MAN: *I rode my horses, drank my wine—*

WOMAN: *The Count of Paris sought my hand—*
MAN: *And I remember Rosaline.*

SCENE V

Main room of the lodgings as before. FRIAR LAURENCE *is still seated, mumbling over his accounts.* ROMEO *enters.*

ROMEO: Still busy, Father? Still with the accounts? I must say, I'm no good at sums at all. . . .

FRIAR LAURENCE: Did you learn nothing in school at all?

ROMEO: Only what all the young men learned: to be a hero. The three R's, a little Latin, and the sonnets of Petrarch. But of business, or accounting—or how to grow old—nothing.

FRIAR LAURENCE [*drily*]: I am aware of that. Seven florins for a cravat!

ROMEO: But isn't it a beauty? Juliet likes it. . . . She's even worse at sums than I am.

FRIAR LAURENCE: The trouble is, my son—we owe either too much, or too little. Too much for comfort—and too little for credit. Ten ducats altogether and. . . .

[*He consults his ledger*]

. . . fifteen florins. It won't do. The moneylenders don't like it.

ROMEO: Ah well—we'll pay them some day when we're home again.

FRIAR LAURENCE: That's not the thing. The thing is, the sum's too small; they doubt if you're a gentleman. A man can borrow only when he owes; the more he owes, the more his credit's good. This was explained to me by His Eminence the Spanish Cardinal-Archbishop in Toledo, that borrowed enough to raise an army to throw the Jews out of Spain. He borrowed from the Jews, naturally. The truth is—you're out of credit, my boy. No one will lend money to a man who owes but ten ducats fifteen.

ROMEO [*nonplused*]: Well—what are we to do?

FRIAR LAURENCE: Do you ever pray, my son?

ROMEO [*uncomfortably*]: Yes . . . now and then. At night, mostly. You know . . . God bless father and mother and the uncles and aunts. . . .

FRIAR LAURENCE [*impatiently*]: Ak! What sort of prayer is that?

ROMEO [*carelessly*]: It's to propitiate them, I suppose. To keep them from eating me during the night.

FRIAR LAURENCE: And do you never go down on your knees humbly before the Lord and say: "Father, forgive me?"

ROMEO: No—so long as Juliet forgives me. I have little sense of other company, Father.

FRIAR LAURENCE [*hurt*]: That statement has little to commend it.

ROMEO [*quickly*]: Beside yourself, that is. . . .

FRIAR LAURENCE [*sourly*]: Thank you for that. You've been too much alone, my boy. The two of you.

ROMEO: Sometimes when we are most together, we are most alone. How is that, Father?

FRIAR LAURENCE: It's man's condition, I suspect. Each of

24

us starts the same—with two eyes, two hands, ten fingers, toes, teeth, and—bones . . . in which he sits in
solitary by himself. And that's his sorrow; that he can
never get anybody to sit in his bones with him. For all
his music and his literature, he's lonely as a cricket. As
to why that should be—I cannot say: our Heavenly
Father must have planned it so. [*Rising, with a sigh*]
Well . . . I suppose I'll have to go to see old Nathan
myself, and let him feel the weight of Holy Church.
I'll try to bring you back a few ducats to ease your
solitary.

[*He goes out.*]

ROMEO [*alone*]: My solitary . . . [*He looks around
helplessly*] Where is everybody? Are we alone in Mantua? Or are we solitary in the world? and the world
solitary in the sky?

Are we alone here, Father, on this earth?
We little few? . . . in all the universe
Alone? No living creature on the stars
That circle through the unexplainèd sky
Like Roman candles? They are multitudes;
And each perhaps as big as Mantua,
With room for creatures . . . and no creatures there?
No one, no thing, no speaking, listening thing
On Mars? On Venus? or on Jupiter?
Or on Orion, or the Polar Star?
Great God, what silence in the firmament!
Our childhood lauds are whispers in the sky,
Too faint for comfort, or too far away.
And youth's hot transports cooled to such a degree
That love, which was the provender I sought
Like a quick sparrow pecking in the Square,

25

Finds me uncertain of my appetite.
For good or ill, I know not—or if God
Is careless of such things—and happiness
Forever and forever but a tale
Told to a child to ease him in the dark.
How large this caverned night in which we sit
Each in his little bag of bones and guts,
Huddled before the fire of the sun,
And crying *Domine!*

                             Aha! But wait!

If so we are alone, why then it seems
That God must have us in some special care,
And must take pleasure in our greening earth,
Having no other but the empty moon,
The barren planets and unlived-in stars
To please His questioning eye. . . . So then it seems
I am by reason of my solitude
In heaven's grace . . .

[A MESSENGER *enters*]

Now now, sir! What is this?

MESSENGER: Please, sir—could you tell me where I might find the young Lord Romeo that was a Montague?

ROMEO: I am Romeo—and still a Montague.

MESSENGER [*staring at* ROMEO's *shabby clothes*]: Oh! Then I've a message from your father, here.

ROMEO [*surprised*]: My father? . . . But you're no Veronese, from your dress. . . .

MESSENGER: No sir. I'm a Venetian. From Venice.

ROMEO [*suspiciously*]: What? Why Venice? From my father, do you say?

MESSENGER: Aye. The old Lord Montague; him with the gout. It comes by way of Venice on account of the old

gentleman being there to visit your aunt the Lady
Claudia on your mother's side, that resides in the afore-
mentioned city.

ROMEO [*impatiently*]:   Never mind all that. Tell me—
what. . . ?

MESSENGER: I don't know what. I was told to give you
this, and that's all I know.

[*He hands* ROMEO *a package.* ROMEO *opens it feverishly;
it contains a bottle.* ROMEO *reads the label incredulously.*]

ROMEO: Sangrelli's Cough Mixture. . . ! A bottle of
cough syrup?

MESSENGER: I guess that's it. We have fine apothecaries
in Venice.

ROMEO [*furious*]:   What kind of joke is this?

MESSENGER: There's a message goes with it. Your father,
the old Lord, he said to me: Alfred, you tell my son
to be of good cheer. He said to tell you he was working for you day and night.

ROMEO [*bitterly*]:   In Venice?

MESSENGER: That's where he's been this Wednesday
month. Came there for the waters. Caught a cold there,
too. [Pointing to the bottle] But that fixed him.

ROMEO: And is that all he sent?

MESSENGER: That, and the three ducats for the usual,
which I have here . . . [*He fumbles in a purse and
produces the coins*] . . . minus one florin three for the
cough medicine. . . .

ROMEO: Damn the cough medicine. Go back to Venice,
and tell my father that the Capulets will get us home,
not he. . . . Commend me to my aunt—and to my
lady mother. . . . How *is* my mother, Alfred, by the
way?

MESSENGER: Why, she does well enough, what with
feeding the pigeons in Saint Mark's every day. A ten-
der-hearted lady, with one of them big hats like a cart-
wheel on her head. She takes her syrups from the same
apothecary as your father.

ROMEO: But—look here . . . if my parents can get to
Venice, why can't they come to Mantua?

MESSENGER: Why, as for that—d'ya see—Verona and
Mantua are at war.

ROMEO [*astonished*]: They are? Nobody told me!
Damme! That's a complication!

MESSENGER: No sir; not for you, sir. Only for the mili-
tary. It's not a declared war—

ROMEO [*impatiently*]: What the devil does *that* mean?

MESSENGER: Well, now, d'ye see, it's a simple matter of
nature, like in the history books, for Mantua is mostly
Guelph . . . or else Ghibelline, I'm not certain which,
but one or the other; and in Verona they're mostly
Ghibelline, as you know, being Ghibelline yourself. Or
maybe 'tis the other way 'round. . . . Ah well, one or
the other, the two cities are at swords' points, but not
in a professional way, mind you, for there's been no
declaration. So you see, sir—it's one of them things.
You're going along thinking your peaceful thoughts—
and all of a sudden—[*He makes a gesture of cutting
his throat*]—zzzzip! *Then* they tell you. Well, I'll be
getting back to Venice. We've got a war on with the
Turks, but we know about that.

[*He goes out.* JULIET *comes hurrying in, hopefully,
doubtfully*]

JULIET: Romy—who was that? . . . Just here . . . ?

ROMEO [*grumpily*]: A messenger.

JULIET [*Could it be?*]:   A messenger? . . . Romy! . . . From . . . ?

ROMEO: From my father.

JULIET [*breathlessly*]:   Oh—Romy!

ROMEO [*shortly*]:   From Venice.

JULIET [*puzzled*]:   Venice. . . ? What. . . ?

ROMEO [*handing her the bottle*]:   He brought me this—

JULIET: What? This. . . ? [*reading*] Sangrelli's . . .

ROMEO: It seems my father is visiting my aunt.

JULIET [*dashed*]:   . . . Cough medicine.

ROMEO [*shortly*]:   He has a cold.

JULIET [*mournfully*]:   Oh, Romy! [*She opens the bottle with indifference, and sniffs at it; then she looks up in surprise*] Why . . . it smells like . . . blackberry jam!

ROMEO: Blackberry jam. . . ?

JULIET: Take a sniff.

[*She holds the bottle out to him; he takes it and sniffs at it.*]

ROMEO: By Saint Francis! It does at that! Have we a glass anywhere? [*He finds a small liqueur glass in* FRIAR LAURENCE'S *cabinet, or desk, and pours out a glass, takes a sip, smacks his lips, and offers it to her.*] It's blackberry cordial!

JULIET [*sipping*]:   Mmmmm. It *is* good, isn't it? Can I drink it even if I *don't* have a cold?

ROMEO [*looking everywhere for another glass—in vain*]:   Father has the gout.

JULIET: He loves you, though, doesn't he. That's something.

ROMEO: He sent me this—from Venice.

JULIET [*sipping*]:   My father never sends me anything.

. . . It must be lovely in Venice now, Romy. It's been so long since we've been anywhere.

ROMEO [*His eyes light on* FRIAR LAURENCE'S *mortar and pestle—he fills the mortar for himself.*]:   There are fleas in the gondolas, my love—or were, when I was young.

JULIET: We picnicked once in Venice, I remember—on the lagoon. In three barges, with lights and music. I was no more than four. It seems we stayed overnight in Padua, with an aunt. I remember the smell of Venice, Romy; it was very strong. But everybody sang, very sweetly. Later, at night, among the lanterns, or so I heard—the ladies danced in dominoes.

ROMEO [*sighs*]:   Ah, yes. . . .

JULIET: There was a lovely place too, in the forest, outside Verona, where we used to go when I was young . . . and where the men would hunt, and the women weave garlands of wild grasses. . . . I think of things like that more and more as I grow older.

ROMEO: Don't say that word. . . !

JULIET: What word?

ROMEO: Older. . . .

JULIET: Oh. . . . That first year, Romy—when we came here—we did have fun, didn't we?

ROMEO [*sighs*]:   Yes. We did.

JULIET: Everything was so . . . I don't know. Even the city looked beautiful sometimes. Mantua. . . .

ROMEO: We hardly saw it. We were in bed mostly.

JULIET [*scandalized—but delighted*]:   Romy! Really!

ROMEO: Well—we were! God!—we were so young, Julie!

JULIET: Do you remember how we danced till dawn, at

the winter festivals? All year long. . . . Do you remember?

ROMEO: I remember. [*They start to dance.*] And the
time you fell into the fountain. In your only good
dress—

JULIET: You pushed me!

ROMEO: I did not! I went in after you . . . I was a
hero!

JULIET: We danced in the fountain for hours. And the
dawn came up, that cool, lemon-colored dawn when
everything's so still and beautiful. . . .

ROMEO: I know. You feel about fifteen years old, and as
tall as a church. And the birds are all singing. . . .

JULIET: The nightingales?

ROMEO: What's the difference? Somebody was. Maybe
me. . . . They came and told us not to dance in the
fountain.

JULIET: Yes. . . . Did we ever do it again after that?

ROMEO: No. There was a water shortage . . . and then
one year you had the influenza. . . . [*They separate*]
. . . and after that. . . . I don't know. . . .

[*They both slump forlornly to the floor;* JULIET *right,*
ROMEO, *left.*]

JULIET [*wistfully*]:   Shall we go dancing again some
day, Romy. . . ? If I still remember how. . . .

ROMEO: Oh come, Julie—it's not that bad! Why—we
danced only a fortnight ago, at the Palace Ball—

JULIET [*with quiet bitterness*]:   Outside, among the link-
boys and the coachmen!

ROMEO: Is it my fault that we were not invited in?

JULIET: That *I* was not invited, you mean? After all, it
was your friend, the Lady Beatrice . . .

31

ROMEO: I've only met her once. Maybe twice.

JULIET: Twice more than I!

ROMEO: That's not my fault. We never entertain. Did you leave cards on the Duke and Duchess?

JULIET: What cards, Romy? We've had no cards engraved. We've nothing to leave. We have no place to entertain in. . . . Look around you! We owe the butcher . . . the vintner. . . . Am I to feed a multitude with five loaves and two fishes?

ROMEO [*crossing himself*]: Juliet! That's blasphemy! . . . You could have sent the Lady Beatrice a note. . . .

JULIET [*bitterly*]: To tell her what? That the young Montagues have been in Mantua these last ten years?

ROMEO [*weakly*]: You could have asked her here to tea. . . .

JULIET [*scornfully*]: With Nurse to serve us crumpets in a dish? What's more—she's *your* friend—not mine.

ROMEO: I swear I've scarce exchanged a word with her. . . . I hardly know the girl!

JULIET [*coldly*]: You said the same of Rosaline.

ROMEO [*impatiently*]: Oh—that was long ago! Besides —she's only visiting here, from her family in Ferrara. . . .

JULIET: I saw your glances in the Square on Saint Bartholomew's Day. And again at early Mass in the Cathedral. . . .

ROMEO: No—truly! On my honor! We met but once . . . or twice . . . at the old Baron's house . . . you know that man . . . what's his name? . . . to do a small part together from a play . . .

JULIET: And said no more together than what was wrote in it?

ROMEO [*stoutly*]:   No more at all. She doesn't even know my name—except perhaps by asking somebody. . . .

JULIET: Oh, marvelous!

ROMEO: By heaven, you do me wrong!

JULIET: That's from another play! Give over, Romy! It *was* the lark, and you were out all night. With whom? The public barber? . . . Besides—the water closet leaks—I just remembered it.

ROMEO [*groaning*]:   Oh—not again!

JULIET [*softening a little—half-mockingly, half-consolingly*]:   Poor Romy! It's hard to cut a figure in the town, knowing at home your water closet leaks.

ROMEO [*glumly*]:   I cut a sorry enough figure as it is.

JULIET [*softening still more*]:   Cheer up, my dear; the closet will be fixed; I'll send Nurse with a message to the smith. Nothing is all that bad. [*A little shyly*] Perhaps tonight we'll walk a little in the Square, and watch the fireworks.

ROMEO: There are no fireworks. . . .

JULIET [*gaily*]:   We'll make our own! Rockets and Catherine-wheels. . . .

ROMEO [*smiling despite himself*]:   And bright Greek fire. . . ?

JULIET: And tomorrow I'll leave a card on the d'Estes. Bother! I had forgot; we have no cards. Well, then— a note. . . . My mother knew the Duchess long ago, in Rimini; they were girls together at the Convent there.

ROMEO [*cheerfully*]:   After all, love, the invitation is much better come from you than from me. . . .

JULIET [*dreamily, pirouetting*]:   I'll wear mother's feather boa. . . .

33

[*A* MESSENGER *enters with a note.*]

Yes? What is it?

MESSENGER: Lord Romeo Montague?

ROMEO [*uneasily*]:   Yes. . . ?

MESSENGER: I have a note for you.

ROMEO: Oh. . . ?

[*He takes the note and reads it; frowns guiltily, and tries to crumple it up.* JULIET *quickly takes it from him, and reads aloud.*]

JULIET: "If you would know my house, 'tis at the tuft of olives here hard by." Signed—B. The d'Este crest . . . a very fancy hand. B is for Beatrice, I presume?

ROMEO [*trying to brazen it out*]:   I've no idea—

JULIET [*She is very calm, and very cold*]:   She does not know your name . . . or where you live. . . .

ROMEO [*blustering*]:   Somebody must have told her. . . .

JULIET: But not yourself. You said no more than what was wrote for a small part in a play. You spoke, but you said nothing. Not "Shall we meet again?". . .

ROMEO: What shall I swear by? By the inconstant moon?

JULIET: Do not swear at all. Never again, by anything. No. [*She looks at him stonily. Suddenly*—] Romeo—I want out!

ROMEO [*startled and a little frightened*]:   Out? What do you mean—out?

JULIET [*from now on with controlled but steadily rising hysteria*]:   I mean *out!*

ROMEO: Juliet!

JULIET: I want out from here. I want out from it.

ROMEO: But . . .

JULIET: I'm tired of it, Romeo. . . . It's over. It's finished. All the sneaky, sniveling little lies. . . . I'm sick

34

and tired of it! I'm finished here. I'm Montague no
more—no more! I'm Capulet! Do you hear? Capulet!

ROMEO [*frightened, but indignant*]:   What do you mean,
Capulet?

JULIET [*dully*]:   Capulet. I would be better dead, dead
in the tomb with Tybalt.

ROMEO: Julie!   **1371932**

JULIET [*she starts to sniffle*]:   Poor dead bones! Give my
feather boa to my mother.

ROMEO [*shocked*]:   Julie! Juliet!

JULIET [*rocking back and forth*]:   Oh willow! willow!

ROMEO: Juliet—please! Don't Julie. . . !

JULIET: What have I left to live for? Tell me that! I
ask you—what?

ROMEO [*hopefully*]:   Why . . . tomorrow! And the day
after. . . .

JULIET: Night after night alone—and you in a tuft of
olive trees!

ROMEO: Now, Julie. . . !

JULIET: False-hearted villain! [*She flies at him and
beats against him with her fists*] I hate you! Do you
hear? I hate you! I despise you!

ROMEO [*seizing hold of her arms*]:   Julie! For heaven's
sake!

JULIET [*crumbling; pitifully*]:   Now look what you've
done! My poor arms! Bruised beyond repair!

ROMEO: I only tried to keep you from . . .

JULIET [*weeping*]:   I'm going to kill myself! Give me
that dagger! I'll sheathe it in my . . .

[*She reaches for the dagger at* ROMEO's *belt, cries, ex-
clamations, ad lib. As he tries to wrest it from her, she
swings a wild fist and hits him in the eye.*]

35

ROMEO [*falling back a step*]:   Ow! Julie! For heaven's
sake. . . !

[JULIET *looks at him in consternation, her wild fury ebb-
ing away.*]

JULIET [*weakly*]:   Romy. . . ?

ROMEO [*wearily, his hand up to his eye*]:   What is it?

JULIET [*mournfully*]:   You don't love me!

ROMEO: I do.

JULIET: No—

ROMEO: I tell you—I do.

JULIET: Then—say it!

ROMEO [*indignantly*]:   At a time like this?

JULIET [*piteously*]:   Lie a little! [*Still more mournfully*]
Romy—

ROMEO: Yes?

JULIET: I'm sorry.

ROMEO [*coldly*]:   Forget it. You fight by the book.

JULIET: Romy . . . I . . . I love you . . .

ROMEO: I know. Not wisely, but too well.

JULIET: Did I hurt you?

ROMEO: What the devil do you think? Of course you
hurt me! I shall have a black eye directly.

JULIET: Oh dear! Let me put a poultice on it! Come . . .

ROMEO: A bit of raw steak, perhaps—

JULIET: We have none—

ROMEO: Liver will do—

JULIET: Oh Romy—we should never have been married! Marriage is such a dreadful thing for young
people!

ROMEO [*wearily*]:   I know; one should start off as grand-
parents to begin with.

JULIET: Here—let me help you, Romy dear.

[*They go out together,* JULIET *leading* ROMEO *by the arm. After a moment the* NURSE *enters, and seeing nobody about, tiptoes to the ledger, opens it, and glances through it with little clucks of disapproval. Then she looks sadly at her old apron, and shakes her head—she will never get a new one! Hearing a noise, she hastily replaces the box, and shuts the drawer. A* MESSENGER *enters from Verona.*]

MESSENGER: Ma'am?

NURSE: And who are you?

MESSENGER: Are you the Lady Montague, that was a Capulet?

NURSE: I was a Capulet, yes . . . not by birth, but by profession. What do you want?

MESSENGER: Nothing with you, then. Is young Lord Montague about?

NURSE: He's about his business; which is none of yours.

MESSENGER: That is as it may be. I have a message for him.

NURSE: Well, give it to me, and I'll see that he gets it. You're a rude young man; but what can you expect from a Mantuan?

MESSENGER: Ma'am, I'm no Mantuan!

NURSE: No Mantuan? Well then . . . what are you?

MESSENGER [*with his finger to his lips*]: Shh! [*He looks about him suspiciously*] I'm from Verona, Ma'am; my life is forfeit if they catch me here. Our two cities being at war.

NURSE: At war? Holy Mother! What next! Well—what's the message? Tell me quickly . . .

37

MESSENGER: The message is for the young Lord Romeo, and his wife, the Lady Juliet.

NURSE: I know . . . I know . . . It's to bid them home —isn't it? Isn't it? I knew it; I knew it. . . .

MESSENGER: The ban is lifted. [NURSE *sinks down, throws her apron up over her head, and begins to scream*] Really, Ma'am . . . calm yourself. Restrain yourself. [*calling*] Ho, in there! We need help here! [*to* NURSE] Can I get you some water?

NURSE [*coming out from under the apron*]: That I've lived to see the day! Oh thank God, thank God! . . . What's the weather like?

MESSENGER: Where?

NURSE: At home, you fool!

MESSENGER: It's been hot. [*She weeps and cries again.*] For heaven's sake, Madam—control yourself. Help! Ho, in there!

[FRIAR LAURENCE *comes running in from one direction, and a moment later* JULIET *appears from the other.*]

FRIAR LAURENCE: What's the matter here? What is it? Nurse—what's the matter? Who are you, sir? What is this?

MESSENGER: I come with a message, Father. Look at her. She's beyond help.

NURSE: . . . It's come, it's come . . .

JULIET: What evil now?

FRIAR LAURENCE: What's come?

MESSENGER [*to* JULIET]: Are you the young Lady Montague, that was a Capulet?

JULIET [*turning pale*]: I am . . . Thank you for the "young"—

NURSE: Oh wurra, wurra . . .

MESSENGER: Then our Lord Escalus, Prince of Verona, bids you and your husband, the young Lord Romeo, to return at once to his domain, to take your place as full citizen and citizeness of that city. . . .

[JULIET *stands silent, pale, with her eyes closed; and sways a little. Then she looks down at her shabby clothes, and makes a sad little gesture.*]

FRIAR LAURENCE: Tell me, good man—to get the story straight; was it the Montague or the Capulet that reached the Prince's ear?

MESSENGER: Why, neither, sir. It was the young girls of the city who have taken to being married among the tombs out of sympathy for the Lady Juliet, and to the disadvantage of the taxpayers.

[ROMEO *enters, holding a piece of liver to his eye, and not altogether dressed.*]

ROMEO [*crossly*]: What's all this screaming and hullabaloo. . . ?

JULIET [*in a small, faltering voice*]: We're going home, Romy.

ROMEO [*thunderstruck*]: Home? . . . Home!

FRIAR LAURENCE: At last.

ROMEO [*pointing to his black eye*]: Home. . . ? With this?

CURTAIN

39

ACT II

~~~~~~~~~~~~~~~~~~~~~~~~~~~~

SCENE I

FRIAR LAURENCE *comes out on stage again as narrator.*

FRIAR LAURENCE: So—we are going home again—after ten years? Ah well; that's no more than a flea bite in eternity—but a lifetime in a family. There have been changes, of course; for one thing, Paris and Rosaline are married; oh—I forgot to tell you: Paris was only wounded in that fight in the graveyard. He always claimed that he slipped just as he was preparing to attack in tierce. He keeps himself quite fit with morning exercises at the window. Deep breathing and so forth . . . the Montagues and the Capulets are still cool to each other. They don't speak—or at least, they speak only when spoken to. But now, of course, with Romeo and Juliet coming home . . . our carriage, by the way, is already at Villafranca. It's not what you'd call a very elegant equipage—in fact, it's a rather seedy barouche. We're all four of us in it—*and* some bedding, and the clothes hampers, of course—not very many of those I'm afraid. . . .

[*He exits as the* CURTAIN RISES *on the Square in Verona; Montague's palace on one side; Capulet's on the other. A*

41

number of posters adorn the walls: "JULIET" (*in large characters*) "*and* Romeo" (*much smaller*). "*Welcome Lovers,*" *and* "*Love Conquers All,*" *and* "*We Shall Overcome.*" *At one side is scrawled in red paint the legend* "*Paolo loves Francesca.*" *Enter* PRINCE ESCALUS *with* SOLDIERS *and* PAPARAZZI. *The* PAPARAZZI *bombard him with questions, to which he makes no immediate reply.*]

PAPARAZZI: Your Highness—when did you decide to recall the lovers?

Why did you change your mind?

Was it the Capulets or the Montagues who . . .

Can you give us a statement on the progress of the war?

How is the weather in Mantua?

Will they be coming in by the north gate, or by the east?

How many young ladies were taken in the cemetery last week?

What is the percentage of suicides by ratio to the number of nubile adolescents?

ESCALUS [*portentously*]:   Gentlemen of the press—

PAPARAZZI: There go the Capulets! Get them! After them! Get the Capulets!

[*The* PAPARAZZI *rush off.* ESCALUS *looks around him at the posters and the graffiti with indignation.*]

ESCALUS: Our dear Verona is a nest of mice!

See how they run to welcome Juliet!

God's blood! You'd think that love was like a cheese,

Good to the last pale crumb.

                         I who possess

By heaven's will this wallèd paradise,

This honeyed city yellow in the sun,

Have had so ripe a rabble at my heels
That all my armored will was overrun,
And dreamt of maidens tripping in the night
To lift their petticoats among the tombs!
A sacrilege. And very damp with dew.
So then Verona's ancient citizens
Did plead with me to cancel my decree
And bring the lovers home. And so I did.
Yet, to a Prince, such ambiguity
Sits like a ball of lemon on the tongue.
This tide of public clamor is too new—
There was no such consent when I was young!
[*He goes off, followed by* SOLDIERS.]
[LORD *and* LADY CAPULET *emerge from their palace and
the* REPORTERS *move in on them.*]
REPORTER: How do you feel, Lady Capulet, now that
your daughter's coming home? I suppose you feel very
happy—
LADY CAPULET: I'm very happy.
REPORTER: What are the plans of the young couple, do
you know?
LADY CAPULET: As yet, I believe, there are no—er—
REPORTER: What's the weather been like in Mantua?
LADY CAPULET: I don't know, I'm sure—I think . . .
REPORTER: Is it true that the Lady Juliet is expecting?
LADY CAPULET [*startled*]: Expecting? What?
REPORTER: That she is in an interesting condition?
REPORTER: Why are they coming home?
LADY CAPULET: Our Lord Prince . . .
REPORTERS: Is it true that Romeo was seen several
nights at the casino with the young Lady Beatrice
d'Este?

Does the Lady Juliet plan to see the County Paris?
Are they going to ask for a separation?

LORD & LADY CAPULET [*spluttering*]:   Really! No—really!
Oh—I say!—

[*They go off behind the Montague palace. The* REPORT-
ERS *reappear as* COUNTY PARIS *and* ROSALINE *cross the
steps.*]

REPORTER: County Paris! County Paris! Are you planning to meet the young Montagues?

PARIS [*pompously*]:   Gentlemen—I'm afraid I can't—er—

REPORTER: What do you think about the new ducal suc-
cession, Count?

PARIS: Really, boys—I can't comment on that—

REPORTER: What about your ambassadorship to Venice?

PARIS: Can't talk about that, gentlemen—

REPORTER: Lady Paris—how do *you* feel about Romeo's
return?

ROSALINE [*embarrassed*]:   Why—how should I feel. . . ?

REPORTER: Weren't you pretty good friends at one time?

ROSALINE: We—knew each other—certainly—

REPORTER: Maybe a little more than that, perhaps?

ROSALINE: Really!

[*The* REPORTERS *leave, laughing.*]

PARIS [*indignantly*]:   Paparazzi!

[*They turn and move off in opposite directions.*]

CURTAIN

SCENE II

─────────────────

The Great Hall at the Montague's Palace in Verona. Romeo's FATHER *and* MOTHER *enter the hall from a side* corridor.

MONTAGUE: I suppose Juliet's folks have gone to meet her. . . .

LADY MONTAGUE: They would. Nine years with their noses in the air; and then they can't wait.

MONTAGUE: What else can you expect from Capulets? . . . What is it, Joseph?

[*A* SERVANT *enters.*]

SERVANT: Lord and Lady Capulet are downstairs, Madam.

LADY MONTAGUE: Oh? Well! . . . Bid them come up, then. [*The* SERVANT *bows, and withdraws.* LADY MONTAGUE *turns indignantly to* MONTAGUE.] Humph! They could at least have gone a little way to meet them! It isn't as though they'd ever lifted a finger for their daughter!

MONTAGUE: Now, Mother—let's be pleasant. After all— she's our daughter-in-law.

LADY MONTAGUE: Humph! She caught him on the rebound from Rosaline—that's all.

MONTAGUE: Now Mother . . .

LADY MONTAGUE: Don't "Mother" me. I know what I know.

MONTAGUE: Well, Rosaline's wed now, to the County Paris. Let's hope there'll be no more trouble.

[LORD *and* LADY CAPULET *enter.*]

CAPULET: Trouble? What trouble? More trouble? I won't have it!

LADY CAPULET: Trouble enough all these years!

CAPULET: Well, Montague. Lady Montague. [*He bows; he is a rough fellow, wealthy and opinionated. The* TWO LADIES *curtsy coolly to each other.*] Well . . . here we are, here we are. I must say—my heart is wondrous light.

MONTAGUE: It's a great day for all of us, I'm sure.

CAPULET: I dare say you'll be glad to see your son again—what? How's your gout, Montague?

MONTAGUE: Well enough, I expect. Took the waters at Mirano. Found a good apothecary, too. Gave me a syrup for my cough.

CAPULET: I have a man in Pisa makes me up a powder of something or other—ergot, I expect.

LADY MONTAGUE [*with a shiver*]:   Don't talk of powders, please! That awful night. . . ! Though *who* took *what* . . . ?

LADY CAPULET: Indeed yes! I have the nightmares thinking of it still. We thought her dead.

CAPULET: Come, Mother. . . !

LADY CAPULET: Well, so we did; and put her in the tomb.

LADY MONTAGUE: [*proudly*]:   And our son took her out.

CAPULET: The young ruffian!

LADY MONTAGUE [*a ruffled hen*]:   To take a dead woman for a wife? A saint!

LADY CAPULET: A saint? At climbing balconies?

46

LADY MONTAGUE [*stoutly*]:   That's no reflection on a growing boy.

MONTAGUE: Come, ladies, come; no need to quarrel now. You wanted Paris, and got Romeo. We wanted Rosaline . . . Well, that's an old story, and ended, too. They're coming home, and that's the main thing.

CAPULET: I wonder has our Juliet grown any stouter. Her mother's family runs a bit to fat.

LADY CAPULET: Humph!

LADY MONTAGUE: I only hope my son's health hasn't suffered.

CAPULET: Why should it, Ma'am? I dare say my Juliet kept table for him.

MONTAGUE [*amiably*]:   Well, anyway—I expect to welcome her as though she were my own.

CAPULET: And I'll greet Romeo like a son. [*The* Two Men *clasp hands.*] [*To his* Wife] Did you hear that, Mother?

LADY CAPULET: I'm more interested in my daughter. It's been ten long years . . . [*Wiping her eyes*] My little girl. I never taught her anything.

LADY MONTAGUE [*firmly*]:   Never mind, my dear. We'll see to that!

MONTAGUE: Hist, ladies . . . I think I hear them . . . at the door . . .

CAPULET: They're here, are they? Dry your eyes, my love.

LADY CAPULET: My poor little girl . . .

[*They all turn toward the door.* ROMEO *and* JULIET *enter, followed by the* NURSE *and* FRIAR LAURENCE. *All move toward one another in a confusion of happy cries and ad lib greetings.*]

47

LADY CAPULET, *weeping, embraces* JULIET. JULIET *embraces her* FATHER. *He holds her out at arm's length, and looks her up and down.*]
The following scene should be played contrapuntally; no pause in the flow and swirl of conversation, with now and then a point made clear as a gull's squawk.]
[*Simultaneous*]

JULIET [*1*]:   Mother!

LADY CAPULET [*1a*]:   Juliet!

JULIET [*3*]:   Father!

LORD CAPULET [*3a*]:   Daughter!

LORD CAPULET [*5*]:   Well well, Julie—a grown woman, by God!

JULIET [*7*]:   You're looking well, Father.

LADY CAPULET [*9*]:   My poor child.

ROMEO [*2*]:   Father!

LORD MONTAGUE [*2a*]:   Son!

ROMEO [*4*]:   Mother!

LADY MONTAGUE [*4a*]:   My boy!

LADY MONTAGUE [*6*]:   Let me look at you! Tst, tst!

ROMEO [*8*]:   Now, Mother!

LADY MONTAGUE [*10*]:   You've lost weight, dear.

LORD MONTAGUE [*11*]:   He's got a bit of a pot, if you ask me!

JULIET [*12*]:   Now, Mother!

LADY CAPULET [*13*]:   You could have written more often.

LADY MONTAGUE [*14*]:   You never wrote, Romy, and all those years.

ROMEO [*15*]:   Oh, Mother.

LADY CAPULET [*16*]:   Whatever have you done to your hair, dear?

48

JULIET [*puzzled, vaguely*] [*17*]:　My hair?

ROMEO [*18*]:　You're looking well, sir! How's the gout?

MONTAGUE [*19*]:　Oh—it kicks up now and then— My right foot, you know.

LADY CAPULET [*20*]:　Do you have to wear it that way?

JULIET [*21*]:　Wear what?

LADY CAPULET [*22*]:　Your hair—

JULIET [*23*]:　Romeo likes it that way.

LADY MONTAGUE [*24*]:　Romy—what's that around your eye?

ROMEO [*25*]:　A bit of yellow, Mother. Liver.

LADY MONTAGUE [*to* MONTAGUE] [*26*]:　I told you he wasn't eating right!

CAPULET [*27*]:　You've filled out a bit, Julie.

JULIET [*28*]:　Have I, Father?

LADY MONTAGUE [*looking over at* JULIET] [*29*]:　Juliet has put on quite a bit of weight, hasn't she?

ROMEO [*30*]:　I hadn't noticed.

LADY CAPULET [*looking over at* ROMEO] [*31*]:　Your husband looks a little seedy, dear.

LADY MONTAGUE [*still looking at* JULIET] [*32*]:　She used to be so slim.

LADY CAPULET [*33*]:　He seems shorter, some- how—

LADY MONTAGUE [*34*]:　I'd scarcely recognize her.

ROMEO [*35*]:　Nonsense, Mother!

LADY CAPULET [*looking at* ROMEO] [*36*]:　He seems to have a few gray hairs—

JULIET [*37*]:　We're older, Mother.

49

LORD CAPULET [38]: By the way, the County
Paris is married.

JULIET [39]: Is he? How nice! To whom?

LADY CAPULET [40]: To Rosaline.

JULIET [*amused*] [41]: To Rosaline? No!

LADY MONTAGUE [42]: Rosaline is married.

LORD MONTAGUE [42a]: To the County Paris.

ROMEO [43]: No! By the Rood!

CAPULET [44]: So you're a Montague now! Hmph!

LADY CAPULET [45]: He asks about you every
time, the County Paris—

CAPULET [46]: He's done very well, Paris.

JULIET [47]: I'm glad.

ROMEO [48]: And how is Rosaline?—The Countess Paris?

LORD MONTAGUE [49]: Oh, fine. They have a big
place at Viareggio.

LADY MONTAGUE [50]: It's very, very grand, dear.

ROMEO [51]: Oh!

CAPULET [52]: Hmph! Hmph! Well . . . I suppose you'll be staying here with the Montagues . . .

JULIET [53]: For a while, I suppose—

LADY MONTAGUE [54]: We've put you in your old
room, Romy.

MONTAGUE [55]: Thought you'd prefer it.

ROMEO [56]: With the single bed?

LADY MONTAGUE [57]: Don't be coarse, dear.
[*crossing to* JULIET] So nice of you to come,
dear. We're so happy to have you—

JULIET [58]: It's so nice of you to have me . . .
Ma'am.

LADY MONTAGUE [*with distaste*] [*59*]:   Really, I
suppose—you should . . . call me . . . Mother.

JULIET [*with difficulty*] [*60*]:   Yes . . . Mother.

LADY CAPULET [*without conviction*] [*61*]:   So
nice of you . . .

LADY MONTAGUE [*62*]:   Would you care to see the
children's quarters?

CAPULET [*63*]:   What for?

LADY CAPULET [*64*]:   Come along, Cappy. [*to*
LADY MONTAGUE] We'd be delighted.

LADY MONTAGUE [*65*]:   Come along then. [*She
leads* JULIET, CAPULET & LADY CAPULET *out,
upper L.*] Their room is just above the rose
garden. Romy used to love to climb in and out
of the window . . .

LADY CAPULET [*66*]:   I'm sure he did . . .

CAPULET [*to* LADY CAPULET] [*67*]:   Fusty old
palace—what?

LADY CAPULET: Hush, Cappy.

[LORD MONTAGUE *and* ROMEO *have been left behind.*]

ROMEO [*looking after the others*]:   It hasn't changed a
bit, has it? [*looking around the room*]:   Still the same
old place.

[LORD MONTAGUE *moves over to him confidentially.*]

MONTAGUE [*embarrassed but eager*]:   I . . . er . . . I've
heard a few stories, my boy . . . here and there, you
know . . .

ROMEO [*carelessly*]   Have you, sir?

MONTAGUE: This—er—Beatrice d'Este . . .?

ROMEO: Oh—that! Nothing to it, Father. We did a little
scene together from *As You Like It*. For some charity affair . . .

51

MONTAGUE: As you liked it, eh? You young dog. [*He sighs*] Ah—to be middle-aged again! [*They leave stage, upper L., following others.* FRIAR LAURENCE *and* NURSE *enter R. and cross stage.*]

FRIAR LAURENCE: Well, Nurse, each to his own, as I expected. Have you had word of your nephew at all?

NURSE: He's gone to America, they tell me, and has become a politician.

FRIAR LAURENCE: Dear, dear; that's a loss.

NURSE: It is, for he was my own sister's child, and it's better to have something in the world belonging to you even if you can't abide the sight of it. Take my mistress now, with her father, that had his foot on her neck ten years ago. "Hang," he said to her; "beg, starve, die in the streets"; and me right there listening, and her mother too, that never said a word. "Baggage," he called her; "Tallow face." And there he is, nuzzling her neck. Men!

FRIAR LAURENCE: Wait 'til they cross-ruff it, Nurse, and try their in-law humors on each other; the Montagues with Juliet, and the Capulets with Romeo. I'll be a candle-holder, and look on.

[*Exit*]

CURTAIN

SCENE III

A bedchamber in the Montague Palace. ROMEO *and* JULIET *are alone, dressing to go out.*

JULIET: It's so strange—being here in your house.

ROMEO: Unhappy, love?

JULIET: I suppose I expected to be in my own little room again, at home.

ROMEO: This is your home now.

JULIET: It was different in Mantua, somehow. I was still a Capulet. Now I'm a Montague. I don't know if I quite like it.

ROMEO [*cheerfully*]: You'll get used to it. After all—we're not such a bad lot!

JULIET [*teasing*]: Aren't you?

[*They embrace.*]

ROMEO: You know—you *have* gotten a little heavy, darling.

JULIET: I'll soon take it off—now that I can ride again. I promised Father to go hunting with him tomorrow.

ROMEO: Without me?

JULIET: Not if you'd like to come. We ride toward Garda.

ROMEO: I haven't been on a horse for years.

JULIET: I expect I'll be sore. But Father's so pleased! It's pathetic, Romy. He's gotten awfully old . . . Darling . . .?

ROMEO: Yes? What is it?

JULIET: Come here a minute . . . Is that a gray hair?
You know—you *are* getting a little gray, my dear . . .

ROMEO [*ruefully*]:   Do you mind, Julie?

JULIET [*gently*]:   Of course not. It makes you look distinguished. [*With elaborate concern*] I was surprised
to hear about our friend Paris—weren't you?

ROMEO: Paris—? Oh . . . yes. And Rosaline . . . of all
people!

JULIET [*lightly*]:   He didn't wait very long, did he, after
all . . . ?

ROMEO [*carelessly*]:   Oh—I don't know. Would you say
so?

JULIET: Wouldn't you, dear?

ROMEO: Rosaline's a very attractive girl.

JULIET: I know. I remember her. I always thought her
rather spinsterish.

ROMEO: They have a place at Viareggio.

JULIET: Naturally!

ROMEO: What do you mean—naturally?

JULIET: I mean—why not? The Parises were always
very well-to-do.

ROMEO: Roz is a very rich girl, on her own, you know.

JULIET: Oh! "Roz"!

ROMEO: Too fair, too wise . . .

JULIET [*icily*]:   Really! Hook me up, please. If you can
reach that high . . .

ROMEO [*as he fastens the back of her dress*]:   What does
that mean?

JULIET [*carelessly*]:   I think you've shrunk a little.

[ROMEO *straightens up, stands on tiptoe, and looks over*
JULIET'S *head at the mirror.*]

JULIET: I like your father. He's rather a dear.

54

ROMEO: He likes you too, I'd say . . .

JULIET: He kissed me.

ROMEO [*drily*]:   I know.

JULIET: He reminds me of you, a little.

ROMEO: Naturally. Chip off the old block. Your mother kissed me, too, as a matter of fact.

[*He grimaces and wipes his mouth with the back of his hand.*]

JULIET: Mother has a very sentimental nature.

ROMEO: I remember when all she wanted was my blood!

JULIET: After all, dear—Tybalt *was* her nephew—

ROMEO: Mercutio was my friend.

JULIET: You know—I never said this to you before— but Mercutio *was* a little trying. . . .

ROMEO: I suppose you preferred Paris.

JULIET [*virtuously*]:   Paris had a very sweet nature.

ROMEO: He was a pompous ass.

JULIET: He was not a pompous ass!

ROMEO [*sulkily*]:   I should have killed him—that day in the cemetery. But my foot slipped. I had no luck at all that day!

JULIET: Really! That's not funny, Romy.

ROMEO: Eh? Oh—sorry, darling. I didn't mean it that way. Look—I'm sure that Paris is a splendid fellow and all that. But—he is a pompous ass.

JULIET: And I say he is not! [*They glare at each other.*] What are you so angry about?

ROMEO: Nothing.

JULIET: I thought once we were home . . .

ROMEO: I know. [*pause*] Were you in love with Paris, Julie?

55

JULIET: Never!

ROMEO [*he kisses her*]:   All right, then. I forgive you.

JULIET: I was in love with springtime and the world.

ROMEO: I know. And summer, and the morning light. It changes, Julie—and that's pitiful.

JULIET: If you were like every other little boy, you were in love with the woman in the moon. Sometimes she wore one face, sometimes another. But always she was shining and pure and true and tender . . . and ninety thousand miles away.

ROMEO: I may still be in love with her.

JULIET: Only—there's no one on earth like that.

ROMEO: Yes there is . . . I married her.

JULIET: You married someone nearer home, Romy. Come—hold her there.

[*She moves into* ROMEO's *arms*]

CURTAIN

SCENE IV

The Great Hall. Enter FRIAR LAURENCE *and* FIRST PAPARAZZI.

PAPARAZZI: The young ladies of the city have heard of your arrival, Father.

FRIAR LAURENCE [*surprised*]:   So?

PAPARAZZI: They are beside themselves.

FRIAR LAURENCE [*mystified*]: In what way?

PAPARAZZI: In the way of all young ladies. They have the desire to scream, and to get married.

FRIAR LAURENCE [*in rebuke*]: I am no harbor-pilot, my friend, ready to steer every stray back into port!

PAPARAZZI: Now there's a salty remark! Were you a sailor, Father?

FRIAR LAURENCE: I was brought up in Genoa.

PAPARAZZI: And sailed the sea?

FRIAR LAURENCE: As far as Rapallo. No, my son; I have but a single aim, to bring a single marriage to safe anchorage. Let the others fly as they please; someone else can keep them from the rocks. I want no more responsibilities. [*There is a sound of shrill screaming off stage.*] What on earth is that? A murder in the Square?

PAPARAZZI: It is the young ladies. They wait for Romeo to show himself.

FRIAR LAURENCE: Good heavens! Do they carry on like that? They'll tear him limb from limb!

PAPARAZZI: They are not very good at climbing balconies. Just as long as he stays out of their reach—

FRIAR LAURENCE [*puzzled*]: I thought it was Juliet who touched their hearts.

PAPARAZZI: Young ladies are touchable all over. [*A loud outburst of screams*] . . . By God, he's down among them! The fool! I'll have to get him out!

[*The* PAPARAZZI *rushes out.* FRIAR LAURENCE *goes to the window and looks out.* SCREAMS *and* CRIES *off.*]

FRIAR LAURENCE:

Oh what a rage of maidens all about!

Those cries ascend from elsewhere than the heart!

They rise from caves of darkness and of time,
And strike with terror our tranquillity.
What!—can these children with their little breasts
Scarcely in bud, make such ferocious din
That gentlemen do tremble in their beds,
And let their hair grow long and learn to lisp?
Can they indeed, against the common good,
Bend an entire city to their will,
Pour scorn on greatness, insult on the past,
And make a hero of a guttersnipe?
Poor Romeo! They press upon his toes!
He runs! He flees! He dodges . . . he escapes!

[ROMEO *enters, out of breath, and considerably rumpled*]

ROMEO [*calling back*]:   Bar the doors! Lock everything!
Call out the guards! Sanctuary! My! Holy Saint Bene-
dict! They all but had me to pieces! Did you hear
them?

FRIAR LAURENCE: I did.

ROMEO [*bewildered*]:   They said they *loved* me! God
save me from such loving!

FRIAR LAURENCE [*doubtfully*]:   But was it really you
they loved? Or Juliet's story?

ROMEO [*uncertainly*]:   Why . . . that . . . They *did*
seem a little disappointed, now that you mention it.
[*indignantly*] What did they expect, Father? A boy of
seventeen? [*He touches his eye*] I swear—several fell
down in a swooning fit before they even laid eyes upon
me! Humph! Idiotic! [*trying to right himself in the
mirror*] You know . . . I *do* look a little gray . . .
around the temples . . .

[LORD *and* LADY MONTAGUE *come hurrying in; the* FRIAR
bows himself out.]

58

LADY MONTAGUE: Romy! What is it? What has happened?

MONTAGUE [*belligerently*]: The Capulets again, eh?

ROMEO: No—no, Father—nothing like that at all. It . . . it was just a—a number of young ladies . . .

LADY MONTAGUE: Oh Romy! Not again! You're married now, dear!

ROMEO: Mother, I swear . . .

LADY MONTAGUE: Don't swear, dear.

ROMEO: Sorry, Mother.

LADY MONTAGUE [*clucking*]: Tsk, tsk, you don't look at all well, dear. I don't think you've been eating right. Is it true what Nurse was telling me—that you lived for a whole season on boiled cabbage?

ROMEO: There was a glut of cabbages one month and the farmers were giving them away. Besides—they weren't always boiled. Sometimes we had them à la Bolognese.

MONTAGUE: That's a gouty diet, my boy. Not healthy at all.

LADY MONTAGUE: You know, dear, I think your Juliet is just a *little* bit spoiled.

MONTAGUE: Now, Mother!

LADY MONTAGUE: Oh—I'm sure she is *well meaning!* But you know, Monty, we've always thought the Capulets a little peculiar. [*to* ROMEO] And I *do* think —and you father agrees with me, dear—that they should be made to share *some* of the expenses. Your father and I are glad to do all we can, but a young woman ought to have *some* kind of dowry, and it isn't as though her parents couldn't afford it . . .

MONTAGUE: On the contrary, dear boy . . . they are very well fixed.

ROMEO: She's talking to her father about that very thing right now, Mother.

MONTAGUE [*heading for the rose garden*]:   Where are they? On the terrace?

ROMEO: In the rose garden, I believe, sir.

MONTAGUE [*stops dead in his tracks*]:   Oops! The rose garden! [*heading in the opposite direction*]: Let's stay out of the thorns as long as possible . . . eh?

[*They go off toward the terrace, followed slowly by* ROMEO.]

SCENE V

On a bench in the rose garden, JULIET, her MOTHER and FATHER.

CAPULET: And I tell you, I will not contribute one penny. I didn't choose this husband of yours; and if I had it to do over again, I wouldn't choose him now, either.

JULIET [*pleadingly*]:   Father . . .

CAPULET: You made your throw; play your point, Julie. Don't ask me to pay the losses.

LADY CAPULET: At least, he's a gentleman, Cappy.

CAPULET: He's not solid. If I thought him so, I'd change my tune.

JULIET: Solid, Father!

CAPULET: Solid. Stuffed, as they say, with honorable parts. I *had* a solid man for you—but you preferred this—this fellow. I consider him a radical.

LADY CAPULET: He *does* carry things off in rather a liberal way, dear.

JULIET: That's why I love him.

CAPULET: Now Julie—we're a conservative family; Capulet men have never had any liberal ideas.

LADY CAPULET: You should have had a child of your own, my dear, long before this.

JULIET: On charity, Mother? In Mantua?

LADY CAPULET [*bustling*]:   Humph! Well!

CAPULET: And another thing . . . Does he always wear such loud cravats?

LADY CAPULET: Exactly. Your father means that for a married man . . .

CAPULET: It's a matter of taste, my dear. Your true gentleman has a taste for simplicity. And that reminds me . . . speaking of a true gentleman—I've invited the County Paris and his wife to ride with us tomorrow.

JULIET: Tomorrow? But I have no proper riding habit!

CAPULET: We'll find you one, my dear. There'll be the four of us; you, me, the Parises—

JULIET: And Romeo—

CAPULET [*sulkily*]:   Oh well—if you want to make a cavalcade of it!

LADY CAPULET: Lady Montague and I will take the wagon, and meet you somewhere for luncheon—and

I'll get Cook to put up a fowl and a green salad—and some little cakes.

CAPULET: Don't forget to pack a flagon of good Asti wine. And a venison pie. I shall go ask the steward if he has some of those long sausages from Bologna. . . .

LADY CAPULET: I shall wear my green alpaca, with a wide hat—and carry an umbrella against the sun.

JULIET: I suppose I could wear my old riding habit . . . if you haven't thrown it away.

LADY CAPULET: It's in your closet at home; we haven't touched any of your things. I can have it let out a little . . .

JULIET: It will have to be let out quite a lot, I'm afraid . . . like everything else . . .

[*They exit.*]

SCENE VI

The hall of the Montagues. ROMEO *is alone, and leaving. As he starts to go, a* SERVANT *enters, bearing a big spray of flowers.* ROMEO *stops him; and looks at it curiously.*

ROMEO: What's this, Peter?
SERVANT: For the Lady Montague, sir.
ROMEO: My lady mother?
SERVANT: Your own young lady, sir.

ROMEO: Really? Well—let me have it. Who's it from?

SERVANT [*handing him the spray*]:   I don't rightly know, Master Romeo; but the man who brought it was dressed in the Paris livery.

ROMEO [*startled*]:   Paris? . . . Is there a card? [*He looks for the card, finds it, and reads the address on it*] "To the Lady Juliet . . ." You're right. Hmm. Well —I'll take it to her.

SERVANT: Yes, sir.

[*He bows and goes out.* ROMEO *stands for a moment in indecision, then he also goes out, carrying the spray.*]

SCENE VII

The rose garden. JULIET *is alone. To her,* ROMEO, *with the wreath.*

JULIET: Hello, dear. I've been having a session with the parents.

ROMEO: I, too. This came for you.

[*He hands it to her.*]

JULIET [*happily*]:   For me? How pretty. Thank you, darling.

ROMEO [*sourly*]:   It's not from me. Thank whoever it is—Paris.

JULIET [*dashed*]:   Paris?

ROMEO: Read the card, and see.

[JULIET *looks at him in perplexity. She takes the card somewhat unwillingly, and reads it slowly.*]

JULIET [*reading*]: "Welcome home. I shall be so glad to ride with you tomorrow. Lord and Lady Paris."

ROMEO [*icily*]: I thought you were riding with your father.

JULIET: I am. He asked the Parises.

ROMEO [*coldly*]: "*I*" shall be so glad. . . .

JULIET: He meant "we" of course. His wife.

ROMEO: He said "I." Besides, I'm not sure Rosaline rides.

JULIET [*coolly*]: Well, then—perhaps you'd rather stay at home?

ROMEO: What does *that* mean?

JULIET: Oh—nothing. I thought it might be fun—to ride out again. Don't you want to, Romy?

ROMEO [*sulkily, looking at the spray*]: Very pretty flowers.

JULIET [*plaintively*]: I thought they were from you.

ROMEO [*bitterly*]: I didn't think of it.

JULIET: Well—it was sweet of him.

ROMEO [*sourly*]: Him!

JULIET [*stubbornly*]: Them!

[*A* SERVANT *enters with a large basket of fruit.*]

SERVANT: Master Romeo. . . ?

ROMEO [*turning*]: Yes?

SERVANT: This was left for you, sir.

[*He gives* ROMEO *the basket, and withdraws*]

ROMEO [*surprised*]: For me?

JULIET [*taking the card, reading*]: For you, dear . . . [*handing him the card*] It's from Rosaline.

[*They stare at each other;* JULIET, *stony-eyed;* ROMEO, *a little defiant—and more than half-pleased.*]

ROMEO: Have a persimmon!

CURTAIN

SCENE VIII

The forest.

[A WOMAN'S VOICE *sings*]:

> *What promises do lovers ever keep?*
> *Only the final promise—to lie deep*
> *Some day in sleep.*
> *To love, to honor, to obey—*
> *That's yesterday!*
> *He cannot even promise to grow old with grace*
> *Or keep some trace of glory on his face.*
> *Something to comfort her, something*
> *To make her think that if the world was lost,*
> *It wasn't lost for nothing.*
> *Dear God, sweet Mary Mother in Heaven above—*
> *If lost my world, as lost it well may be—*
> *Let it be lost for love!*

[FRIAR LAURENCE *comes on stage as narrator.*]

FRIAR LAURENCE: We are in a forest glade outside Verona. We could just as easily be in the vale of Sharon

when Solomon was in Jerusalem, or in the forests of
Fontainebleau. The ladies have been riding—or at
least, some of them have; the gentlemen have been
hawking; and now they are at table. It is a bucolic
scene, somewhere between a Renaissance tapestry and
a cook-out in the Catskills. Of course, you'll have to
use your imagination . . . but then, you've all been on
family picnics before, haven't you . . . ? The surface
is sunny and shining, like a lake; and underneath, the
fish are eating one another. The temperature is warm,
the air is humid, and there is thunder somewhere be-
low the horizon. It is very hard to grow up and to
keep a high heart. Of course, some people never grow
up. They are the fortunate ones; they die young, and
make our poetry. It's easier, really . . .

[*He leaves the stage.*]

[*A woodland grove near Asti.* FRIAR LAURENCE *and*
NURSE *are busy tending a small fire downstage R;* ROMEO
is with them. FRIAR LAURENCE *is frying sausages; there
are wicker food hampers nearby. A wagon is seen in the
background; a little to one side is a rustic table around
which are seated in order:* JULIET, LADY MONTAGUE, LORD
MONTAGUE, LADY CAPULET, LORD CAPULET, ROSALINE,
and COUNTY PARIS. *All are in riding costume, except the
two ladies* CAPULET *and* MONTAGUE, *each of whom car-
ries a parasol. . . . Two hawks (stuffed), hooded, and in
jesses, perch on the low, stripped branch of a small tree.
Those seated around the table are eating and drinking,
and making conversation, in good spirit; it is general conversation at first.*]

ROMEO [*crossing upstage; to* LADY CAPULET]:   Can I
offer you a little more salad . . . Mother?

LADY CAPULET & LADY MONTAGUE [*together*]: No thank you.

[*They turn and glare at each other.*]

JULIET [*to* LADY MONTAGUE]: It has turned out such a lovely day.

LADY MONTAGUE [*to* JULIET]: Has it not? I am so glad I brought my parasol.

MONTAGUE [*to* CAPULET]: A very decent wine, this. Unassuming, of course, but ingratiating—

CAPULET [*to* MONTAGUE]: I got it from a little man in Padua.

PARIS [*to* ROSALINE]: Have you had a sausage, my dear?

ROSALINE [*to* PARIS]: I taste them for days afterwards.

PARIS [*to* JULIET]: A very nice place, this—

JULIET [*to* PARIS]: We used to come here often when I was a girl.

PARIS: Ah yes. No doubt.

CAPULET [*to* MONTAGUE]: A touch more wine?

LADY MONTAGUE [*to* MONTAGUE]: I think you've drunk enough, Monty.

CAPULET [*to* LADY MONTAGUE]: It's a mild vintage, Ma'am.

LADY MONTAGUE [*to* LADY CAPULET]: He has to watch his bladder, I'm afraid.

LADY CAPULET: That reminds me . . . [*She rises a bit unsteadily, and starts off R.*] That way, would you say?

JULIET [*also rising*]: I'll come with you, Mother.

[JULIET *and* LADY CAPULET *go off R.*]

LADY MONTAGUE [*rising*]: I believe that I am also reminded . . .

[*She follows them off.*]

[PARIS *and* ROSALINE *also leave, L.;* LORD MONTAGUE, *left at table, falls asleep;* FRIAR LAURENCE *and the* NURSE *go off.* CAPULET *and* ROMEO *come downstage L.*]

CAPULET [*to* ROMEO]:   Well—you'll have a little more, I guess . . .

ROMEO: Thank you, sir.

CAPULET [*genially*]:   You young fellows—you don't have to think about your kidneys.

ROMEO: I'll have to soon enough, I'm afraid.

CAPULET: I dare say. Well—how do you like being married, eh?

ROMEO: I find it quite tolerable, sir. We pity each other; and we amuse each other sometimes.

CAPULET: Humph! That's a devilish strange view of marriage! Far out indeed! Very modern, I must say!

ROMEO: And what would *your* view be, sir?

CAPULET: The Lady Capulet does *not* amuse me—for one thing. And if I found she pitied me—by God, I'd wring her neck!

ROMEO: Well—there you are, sir. Woman is a pretty puzzle, is she not? No doubt it was planned that way.

CAPULET: Mmm. And what are *your* plans, young man?

ROMEO: Why, sir, I have middle-aged plans; which is to say, neither too hopeful nor too critical.

CAPULET: You're not going to live with your parents forever—are you?

ROMEO: I lack the means to set up an establishment of my own, sir. [*Plaintively.*] Besides—I've only just got home.

CAPULET: Well . . . what did you do in Mantua all those years?

ROMEO [*blankly*]:   Do?

CAPULET [*testily*]:   Do. You did do some sort of business, I suppose?

ROMEO: I'm afraid not, sir . . . not being trained for it, for one thing—and being, so to speak, a foreigner in the city . . .

LORD CAPULET: Ah well . . . you made some contacts, I dare say—of a useful nature . . .

[*Goes back to the table and picks up his austringer's glove, starts to put it on.*]

ROMEO: Alas . . . no. We didn't entertain very much. Your daughter was not always prepared for company— feeling herself unliked, and unattractive.

CAPULET: Unliked? That's odd! Juliet? And unattractive? I never thought her so. D'you find her unattractive?

ROMEO: Good God, no! Juliet's the sun! . . . We—we lived quietly from choice, that's all. We . . . preferred each other's company.

CAPULET [*crossing down*]:   Not very forward-looking, I would say.

ROMEO: You come upon me a little late, sir—to be for-ward-looking. I was my father's son, with the usual expectancies; and then I was ten years in banishment, living upon cabbages. Now I'm my father's son again. Give me leave to draw breath and look around me.

CAPULET: A shaky structure, Montague; shaky. It leans, like Pisa's tower. A father wants his daughter married to a solid man. Take young Paris there! [*As* PARIS *en-ters L. and goes to the table.*] He's solid as a nut. Four children, two hundred head of cattle, and a sardine factory at Portofino. [*pause*] I hear you play at cards.

ROMEO: Yes—if you could call it playing. I find it less than gay . . .

CAPULET [*taking his hawk on his wrist*]:   It's time you
were settling down, my boy. You're getting on, you
know. We all are, for that matter.

ROMEO: You're right, sir; we're getting on. And toward
what goal? I mean to say—with what ahead?

CAPULET: Why—heaven, I expect; or so they tell us in
church . . .

[*He crosses down and exits lower L.*]

ROMEO [*half-aside—but quite clearly*]:   Good God, sir
. . . shall we meet in heaven, too?

[ROMEO *exits lower R. as* JULIET *enters from upper R.*]

PARIS [*he is a ruddy, somewhat pompous, and well-satis-
fied young-old man*]:   You are looking wonderfully
well, Juliet. Odd—when I saw you last, you were
scarcely more than a girl; and here you are, a woman
grown.

JULIET [*ruefully*]:   Grown out, you mean . . . A little
too fully?

PARIS: No, no—I mean no such thing! I protest! I find
maturity very agreeable in a woman.

JULIET: You're very kind. But then—you always were.

PARIS: It was never any trouble to be kind to you, Juliet.

JULIET: I've had no chance to thank you for the flowers—

PARIS: I protest—it was a pleasure . . .

JULIET: Please—don't protest! You always did, you
know—

PARIS: Protest? No—really! Now I *do* protest.

JULIET: There—you see? [*Leaning over and placing her
hand for a moment on his*] Never mind—I rather like
it. One rather misses a certain kind of—gallantry, after
a while . . .

PARIS: It's only the way I feel, Juliet.

JULIET: Don't ever change, my dear. So much changes in the world—one must cling a little to the past—

[LADY MONTAGUE *enters.*]

LADY MONTAGUE: My dear—do you think it wise to be in the sun so long without a sunshade?

JULIET: We're shadowed here, Mother Montague.

LADY MONTAGUE: One never knows. It's very treacherous, the sunlight. I know a woman who went out in the sun without a hat; and her skin turned black. [ROSALINE *enters upstage R.*] I always carry something in my reticule when I go out.

PARIS: Excuse me.

[*He and* ROSALINE *exit lower L.*]

JULIET: Perhaps we are more used to it nowadays. We have been so long in a hard light.

LADY MONTAGUE: My son tells me that your digestion is delicate . . . ?

JULIET [*surprised*]:   Did he? How strange; I wonder why. We ate but lightly, Ma'am.

LADY MONTAGUE: Perhaps I misunderstood him. He says that he brings you breakfast in bed . . . or am I wrong?

JULIET: That's true.

LADY MONTAGUE: I'm afraid he is inclined to spoil you, my dear. Montague men always spoil their women. I breakfast every morning with my husband; he likes me to prepare his chocolate for him.

JULIET: Romeo was not often home for breakfast, Ma'am. We met, usually, at noon.

LADY MONTAGUE [*nodding wisely*]:   If a man stays out,

he has a reason for it . . . I always say a woman
makes a home . . . don't you think?

JULIET [*dutifully*]:   Yes Ma'am.

LADY MONTAGUE: And a marriage . . . ?

JULIET [*reciting, a little awkwardly*]:   I have read—that
marriage is a series of little shocks—any one of which,
like an apoplexy, can kill you.

LADY MONTAGUE [*startled*]:   Little shocks! [*reflectively*]
Yes . . .

JULIET [*as herself again, warmly*]:   But if you love your
husband, you survive.

LADY MONTAGUE [*still at a loss*]:   I suppose so. Young
people seem to survive almost anything these days.
The Parises have four children. [*This appears to be a
non sequitur, but it is not.*] Still, they seem to entertain
a good deal. The d'Estes have dined there, and the
Medicis.

JULIET [*rallying forlornly*]:   The d'Estes were in Mantua, visiting.

LADY MONTAGUE: Yes—I collect that my son was a
friend to the Lady Beatrice. You entertained her,
of course?

JULIET [*bravely*]:   I know the Lady Beatrice very well.
Her mother and my own were at school together.

LADY MONTAGUE: Then you attended the Cotillion at the
palace . . . ?

JULIET: Alas—it seems I could not get my gown in
time. I had a little woman—truly a genius, a sweet
dressmaker—but she was ill, and all the others being
spoken for— And of course Romy would never dream
to go without me. We were obliged to make our ex-
cuses. [*as an afterthought*] I had a cold, besides.

LADY MONTAGUE [*not fooled at all*]:   Of course, my dear.
I understand! You must ask Rosaline for the address
of her dressmaker. Rosaline had such exquisite taste.
[*confidentially*] The Prince is much taken with her;
her husband may be named Ambassador to Venice.
[*She and* JULIET *rise and start out R.*]

JULIET [*coolly*]:   He has a great deal to be grateful for,
has he not!

LADY MONTAGUE: Well—she *had* a considerable dowry
of course—she brought him several large farms, a
winery and, I believe, a villa in Viareggio.

JULIET: She was an orphan, too.

[JULIET *and* LADY MONTAGUE *exit R.*—ROSALINE *and*
PARIS *enter upper L.*]

ROSALINE: I wish I knew how the children are . . .

PARIS [*he is a little tired of saying the same thing*]:
They're all right, my dear.

ROSALINE: I know . . . But that cough of Joseph's. I
shouldn't have come today.

PARIS: Stop worrying, my dear.

ROSALINE: It isn't as though we still had Maria with
us. I could trust her absolutely anywhere. I don't think
this new girl knows anything.

PARIS: Why did you take her, then?

ROSALINE: They're so hard to get, dear. I was glad to
get *anyone*. And she was highly recommended by your
cousin Delia. . . .

PARIS [*impatiently*]:   Oh! Delia! That idiot!

ROSALINE: Well, after all, she *is* your cousin, dear . . .
She's the one that sent us that laundress—the one that
was so good—remember? I wish I could make up my

mind whether to put the green damask chairs in the dining room, or the red velvet. . . .

PARIS [*wearily*]: Yes, dear.

ROSALINE: I wish you were a little more help to me! It's so hard to decide all these things by myself . . . And I'm so afraid it might be the croup!

PARIS: What might be—for heaven's sake?

ROSALINE: Joseph's cough.

PARIS: Are you going to spend the entire day worrying about Joseph's cough?

ROSALINE: I can't help it; someone has to. He could choke to death. And Dr. Heifitz is in Firenze.

PARIS: Ah well . . . I dare say it will be all right.

ROSALINE: I wish I'd worn my yellow riding habit instead of this old thing . . .

PARIS: I thought it had just come in from London—

[NURSE *enters, goes to table.*]

ROSALINE: I wish I hadn't come today. I wish I'd stayed home.

PARIS: I do protest! Try to make the best of it!

ROSALINE: I can't eat sausage; it disagrees with me.

[*The* NURSE *offers* ROSALINE *a bowl of fruit, which* ROSALINE *declines.*]

ROSALINE [*glancing up*]: No thank you—

[*Rises and exits down L.*]

PARIS [*rises*]: My wife can't eat fruit. She breaks out in hives.

[*follows* ROSALINE *off.*]

[NURSE *draws back, offers fruit to* LADY CAPULET *and* LADY MONTAGUE *as they enter.*]

NURSE: Ladies—

LADY MONTAGUE: No, thank you.

LADY CAPULET: Thank you.

74

[*She takes a piece of fruit.* N U R S E *leaves R.*]

LADY MONTAGUE: Your Juliet is very sweet.

LADY CAPULET: Thank you. We did our best for her.

LADY MONTAGUE: Of course, she was very young when they—er—

LADY CAPULET: She was a child.

LADY MONTAGUE: So was my Romeo. A mere boy . . . I suppose that you and Juliet were—very close?

LADY CAPULET [*lying*]:   Oh yes. We were . . . very close.

LADY MONTAGUE: My mother and I were very close. When I married Montague, she made me a present of all her recipes. Veal Parmigian, chicken cacciatore, scampi, cabbage à la Bolognese . . .

LADY CAPULET [*with loathing*]:   Very nice. Very tasty.

LADY MONTAGUE: Tell me . . . what were you planning to give *your* daughter, Lady Capulet? As a wedding present?

LADY CAPULET: Isn't it a little . . . late for a wedding present? I mean to say . . . ten years. . . ?

LADY MONTAGUE: Ten years. Ah, yes. That's china, I believe.

LADY CAPULET: China?

LADY MONTAGUE: The tenth year, you know. It's customary to give china . . .

LADY CAPULET: What would they do with dishes . . . having nowhere to keep them—?

LADY MONTAGUE: Exactly. Therefore.

LADY CAPULET [*uneasily*]:   Therefore what? I'm afraid you've lost the throw, Lady Montague.

LADY MONTAGUE [*puzzled*]:   The throw?

LADY CAPULET [*uncertainly*]:   I'm not certain . . . It's . . . it's a gambling term, I believe. My husband . . .

LADY MONTAGUE: How quaint. The throw . . . I must

remember that. However—All mothers gamble, don't you think? That their sons will marry to their wishes? Some girl of noble family . . .

LADY CAPULET: Of course.

LADY MONTAGUE: With a proper dowry?

LADY CAPULET: Oh. [*ruffling her feathers*] Like Rosaline, perhaps?

LADY MONTAGUE: Indeed, like Rosaline.

LADY CAPULET: Romeo is no County Paris, Madam!

LADY MONTAGUE: He is a Montague. I married a Montague myself, Madam.

LADY CAPULET: So you did. I married a Capulet. So did your son, I believe.

LADY MONTAGUE: And your daughter married a Montague . . . if I am not mistaken.

LADY CAPULET: Unfortunately . . .

LADY MONTAGUE: Unfortunately.

[*The* TWO LADIES *stare stonily into space.*]

SCENE IX

Another part of the forest. LORD MONTAGUE *and* LORD CAPULET *are walking together, gazing at the sky.*

MONTAGUE: Is that your hawk or mine, up there?

CAPULET: Yours, I think. The tail looks a bit pinched.

MONTAGUE: My bird's a bit on the old side, I'm afraid.

CAPULET: It happens to us all.

MONTAGUE: She was downy as a pigeon when I first had her. A sweet little tuft.

CAPULET: Was she plucked?

MONTAGUE: Regularly. When she wasn't in moult.

CAPULET: Keep 'em in the air, I always say.

MONTAGUE: They won't fly when they're in moult. Where did you get yours, Capulet?

CAPULET: Got her from a little man in Ravenna. [*He puts a silver whistle to his lips and blows. He motions impatiently at the bird in the sky.*] Hoy!

MONTAGUE: Fact is, I haven't flown a hawk in years. Never could get the silly creature not to bate. Gave it up, finally.

CAPULET: You've got to be like a husband to her—firm and easy. She'll not bate.

MONTAGUE: You think it easy to be a husband?

CAPULET: Nothing is easy in this world, my friend—nor to be a father, either. But I've been tender—though my fingers itched—

MONTAGUE: D'you mean to settle something on your girl, Capulet?

CAPULET: Well, now . . . That would bear thinking of. You have something in mind for your son, my friend?

MONTAGUE: I've paid out three good ducats a month these last ten years—since you ask—

CAPULET: So you have. It was your son that found himself in Mantua.

MONTAGUE: With your daughter, Capulet.

CAPULET: She could have had a solid man, except for him.

MONTAGUE: My boy is solid enough—or would be; with a proper dowered wife—

CAPULET: That is as it may be. Fly your hawk, Montague—and let me fly my own. [*Calling to his hawk*]
Come girl! Stoop to it!

[*They exit in opposite directions.*]

SCENE X

***

Another part of the forest. JULIET, ROMEO, ROSALINE, *and*
PARIS *are strolling together. They come to a tree that bars
their way;* PARIS *holds back a branch for the others to
pass.* JULIET *and* ROSALINE *step through together.*

ROSALINE: I love the woods, don't you? The air is so re-
freshing.

JULIET [it is not a question]:   Is it the hunt you love,
Lady Paris . . . ?

[*Again* PARIS *holds back a branch for the others to pass.*
JULIET *steps through, but* ROSALINE *manages to drop her
reticule, and as she stands and waits for* ROMEO *to pick
it up,* PARIS, *wearied of holding the branch, lets it fall,
with himself and* JULIET *on the other side.* ROSALINE
stands smiling at ROMEO; *then, still smiling, she starts off
in quite another direction.* ROMEO *hesitates a moment,
then follows her.*]

ROSALINE: Tell me . . . Was it very bad in Mantua?

ROMEO: Yes—it was bad—

ROSALINE: It would seem strange to live in a foreign
land.

ROMEO: To be in exile is not to be in another land, but in another world. The moon gives a different light, and birds sing other songs. And people wear strange faces, and use foreign words. Even the flowers are different; and church bells make a lonely sound. One lives with memories . . . which die each day a little.

ROSALINE: I was so sorry for you.

ROMEO: Thank you, Roz.

ROSALINE: Did you ever think of me in Mantua?

ROMEO: Yes.

ROSALINE: I thought of you often.

ROMEO: I never knew it.

ROSALINE: And if you had?

ROMEO [*lightly*]:   It would have marvelously sweetened the air between Verona and Mantua!

ROSALINE: I suppose I shouldn't have come today.

ROMEO: Why? I'm glad you did.

ROSALINE: Are you?

ROMEO: Of course.

ROSALINE: Are you happy, Romeo?

ROMEO [*flatly*]:   Yes—I'm happy.

ROSALINE: I want you to be, you know.

ROMEO [*touched*]:   Why—that's good of you, Roz.

ROSALINE: I was always a little afraid of you, you know.

ROMEO [*smiling*]:   I didn't know.

ROSALINE: I still am—a little . . .

ROMEO [*still lightly*]:   Then the years have done less damage than I thought!

ROSALINE: I see no damage—a trace of silver in your hair. I find it rather romantic . . . You were always the most attractive man I'd ever met . . .

ROMEO [*remembers that* JULIET *said that to him once*]: Was I?

ROSALINE: You still are.

ROMEO: Why—thank you—

ROSALINE: No . . . It's—just that you've made me remember something that was very sweet . . . and that I
thought I'd forgotten . . . Something . . . long ago.
When I was young. I was happy then. I was in love
with springtime, and the world—

ROMEO: I know. There is a kind of shining in the past;
sometimes a trace of it steals over to the present, and
for a moment makes it sorrowfully sweet. I hunt those
moments, Rosaline—like a greedy child . . . I suppose
I *am* a greedy child—

ROSALINE [*dreamily*]: Oh—to be children, Romeo, and
in love . . .

ROMEO: No one's a child for long—

ROSALINE: . . . [*pause*] Do you think I am a huntress,
Romeo?

ROMEO [*lightly*]: A huntress? Am I your quarry, Roz?
Careful! I might not try too hard to run away!

ROSALINE [*a little breathlessly*]: Perhaps I don't want
you to!

ROMEO [*flatly*]: You did once.

ROSALINE: I didn't think you'd go so far!

ROMEO: I thought you'd broken my heart—for a day or
two.

ROSALINE [*teasing*]: Wasn't there even a tiny scar left
over?

ROMEO [*quoting*]: He jests at scars who never felt a
wound!

ROSALINE [*pouting*]: Now you're laughing at me!

ROMEO [*ruefully*]: Am I, Roz? No . . . at myself. I'd
forgotten it!

ROSALINE: I hadn't. It's all that's left of springtime isn't it? What we remember?

ROMEO [*casting about*]:   I wonder where the others are . . .

ROSALINE [*closing in*]:   Do you care? I don't.

ROMEO [*uncomfortably*]:   No . . . but aren't we getting a little. . . ?

ROSALINE: I wish it wasn't quite so much the way it used to be . . . for me.

[ROMEO *begins to back away;* ROSALINE *follows.*]

ROMEO: Is it . . . Roz?

ROSALINE: I wish . . .

ROMEO: Roz . . .

ROSALINE [*desperately*]:   I wish you'd kiss me . . . once . . . for springtime's sake. I'd like to think I was attractive . . . to *some*body . . . still! And don't say I protest! Ten years, Romy!

[ROMEO *has backed offstage,* ROSALINE *following him.*]

SCENE XI

Another part of the forest. PARIS *and* JULIET *are walking together.*

PARIS: It must have been very trying to be obliged to live so long abroad. I dare say one misses one's parents.

81

JULIET: Of course. But home is more than that.

PARIS: Might I dare believe that you missed your . . . friends?

JULIET [*simply*]:   Why not? Home is a nest of child-hood, with all its memories. You have been very suc-cessful, haven't you? I'm glad.

PARIS: I've done fairly well; as you know, I have four charming children, though one of them, I believe, has the croup.

JULIET: Have you tried honey and wine?

PARIS: Wine?

JULIET: And honey.

PARIS: Why . . . I don't know. I must ask Rosaline.

JULIET: It's an old remedy; she probably knows it.

PARIS: As I say, I've done fairly well . . . And of course, Rosaline has been an ever-present help. I should be less than fair not to give her credit. You heard, per-haps, that I was to be named Ambassador to Venice?

JULIET: I'm so glad for you!

PARIS: Yes . . . Well . . . It was my dream to take you there some day.

JULIET: It's a beautiful city, they tell me.

PARIS: Why did you, Juliet?

JULIET [*puzzled*]:   Why did I . . . ?

PARIS: . . . It's strange the way things happen. I wonder if they always happen for the best.

JULIET: I wish I knew. . . .

PARIS: You think they only happen to try us?

JULIET: There is so much in the world that I wonder about— [*she feels her chin with the back of her hand; could there be the beginning of a double chin? Then, turning to him brightly*] . . . Tell me about your chil-

dren, Paris. You have—how many?—four? Are they
like you? or—or Rosaline?

PARIS: Would you care to see—? [*He takes out a minia-*
ture, and shows it to her.] That's Joseph. And that's
little Katherine. She's two.

JULIET: She has your eyes. And her mother's chin . . .
[*after a pause*] I feel very sad, Paris. . . .

PARIS [*upset*]:   Sad? . . . But you mustn't feel sad, Juliet!
I can't bear to think of you sad. . . .

JULIET: What does a woman do when she feels old—
and unattractive?

PARIS: You? Old? That's ridiculous!

JULIET [*wearily*]:   Ten years is a long time, my dear, to
stay young . . . in Mantua.

PARIS: Ah—long indeed! Juliet, I wasn't going to tell
you this! All these years you've never been out of my
thoughts . . .

JULIET [*surprised and touched*]:   Truly?

PARIS: On my honor!

JULIET: Dear Paris! It is nice to be remembered!

PARIS: Remembered? How much more! You must ever
seem to me that same sweet child you were!

JULIET: A child . . . Yes, I suppose I was. Not too wise
. . . And yet, it warms my heart a little. [*Shyly*] Am I
still . . . ?

PARIS: Sweet? I do protest, you are!

[*He kisses her hand.*]

JULIET [*Lets her hand rest for a moment in his. She is*
enjoying herself—but only for a moment. Then,
firmly]:   I'm not a child any longer, Paris. I think—
perhaps—it's time to join the others.

PARIS: So soon?

JULIET [*lightly*]:   They'll think us lost . . .

PARIS [*recklessly*]:   The whole world lost for . . .

JULIET [*quickly placing her hand against his lips to stop him*]:   No, Paris dear—not that.

PARIS [*embarrassed, and a little sulky*]:   I forgot myself. Forgive me.

JULIET: With all my heart. Now, really, we must go.

PARIS [*formally*]:   If ever I can help you, Juliet . . . if ever I can do anything for you . . .

JULIET: Just hold the branches back from my face. . . .

[PARIS *and* JULIET *turn back through the forest;* PARIS *reaches for a branch, to bend it out of the way.*]

PARIS: Joseph has the croup. [*He parts the branch and he and* JULIET *step through, to confront* ROMEO *and* ROSALINE *who are discovered embraced. They not unnaturally fly apart.*] By God! Rosaline!

[JULIET *stands absolutely still, staring at what she often feared—yet never really believed. Her heart is broken, and the pieces show like eggshell on her face.*]

ROMEO [*miserably*]:   Oh Lord!

[ROSALINE *lays a hand on his arm to restrain and comfort him.*]

PARIS: I am very much surprised at this, Rosaline. I don't know what to say to you.

ROSALINE: Then the less said, the better, Paris.

PARIS [*to* ROMEO]:   As for you, sir—I consider that you have treated a gentle and lovely lady in a most shameful manner.

ROMEO: I crave your pardon, Paris. [*Turning in anguish to* JULIET] Julie!

PARIS: You are a villain, sir. As for my pardon, it is not mine to give. Ask it of the lady.

ROMEO: Villain am I none. But let's not quarrel—*now.*
Not again. [*To* ROSALINE] I ask your pardon, Lady.

PARIS [ROMEO *has turned to the wrong lady*]: No! Not
her!

ROSALINE: You might have left me my pride. It shames
me to have to grant forgiveness for what I did enjoy.

JULIET: Did ever dragon keep so fair a cave?

PARIS: I say! Really, Rosaline—!

ROMEO: Paris, I will be glad to give you satisfaction for
whatever wrong I have done your wife.

[JULIET *turns and walks proudly and fiercely and a little
blindly—away.*]

ROMEO [*crying out after her*]: Julie!

PARIS: It is to your own wife you should apologize, sir
. . . not mine. It is what you have done to Juliet that
I resent!

ROMEO [*astounded*]: Juliet? *You* resent. . . ?

PARIS [*stoutly*]: I do!

ROMEO: Now what the devil is my wife to you?

PARIS: More than I'd care to say.

ROSALINE: Well!

ROMEO: Oh? . . . That puts a different marker on the
green. Indeed!

PARIS: Make no mistake, sir. Your wife is virtue itself.

ROMEO: I need no one to tell me that, sir. But you—?
Are you also virtuous? Or do you crawl with hunger,
like a snake on its belly? Or are you a fox, behind a
husband's back?

PARIS: A coward's back, sir.

[*He offers* ROSALINE *his arm.*]

ROMEO: Now Paris, take the villain back you lately gave
me! [*He steps forward and slaps* PARIS.] That is for

my wife, sir. For keeping her too long in the woods.

ROSALINE [*faintly*]:   Oh . . . !

PARIS [*stiffly*]:   You will hear from me, sir.

ROMEO [*bowing*]:   At your service . . . [*Calling*] Juliet
. . . !

[*He rushes off*]

PARIS [*calling after him*]:   My seconds will wait upon
you, sir.

[*Not looking at* ROSALINE, *he stalks off.*]

ROSALINE [*alone*]:   Oh, never was a story of more woe!

ROMEO [*offstage*]:   Juliet!

[*Offstage bird-call: Cuckoo! Cuckoo!*]

CURTAIN

ACT III

SCENE I

FRIAR LAURENCE [*As narrator*]:

> "*Now, ere the sun advance his burning eye,*
> *The day to cheer, and night's dark dew to dry,*
> *I must up-fill this osier-cage of ours. . .* "

The truth is, we're in the pickle barrel again. Who was
it said, of man's whole history: "He was born, he lived,
he suffered, and he died"?

[*He genuflects*]

> "*Requiem aeternam dona eis, Domine.*"

Still—this is a comedy, my friends—not a tragedy. Of
course, it's easy, looking back, to see things as comic
which were really bitter brine at the time. And there's
much trouble here. The County Paris isn't speaking to
his wife; and where is Juliet? Nobody knows. She has
gone off by herself—disappeared, as it were, into her
own heart's anguish. It's a way women have of re-
proaching heaven for having put men in the world.
Some say it with a blow, some with a sigh soft as the
murmur of a writer's pen. And that's our Juliet. The
girl is gone. . . . We seem to have made a botch of it

87

again! . . . Well, as the poet says, I have things to do
before I sleep.

>Man treads a squirrel cage of grief and glory.
>No matter how he runs, some ghostly doom
>Can catch him like a fog. This certain story
>Can end where it began, in Juliet's tomb.
>God give me strength to comfort and assist—
>Couch Romeo, and play the analyst!

[He exists, sighing]

[*A* WOMAN'S VOICE *is heard singing*]:

>*I was in love with the summer's gold,*
>*But the days come and go;*
>*And the willow leaves turn brown and old,*
>*And the wind is cold, and my heart is slow*
>*To follow morning, for evening shadows*
>*Come stealing over, over, over. . .*
>*I have lost the world and its golden meadows*
>*Not for love, but a faithless lover.*

[*A Square in Verona—night.* JULIET *is seated on the rim
of a fountain or stone bench huddled mournfully in her
feather boa. The* PAPARAZZI *go by without noticing her.*]

PAPARAZZI NOS. 1 & 2:   So the Montagues and the Capulets are at it again! Not so—it is Paris and the young
Romeo. Young, you say? Well, young enough, but not
so young enough! Paris is a Capulet only by indirec-
tion, having been affianced to Juliet. But not married;
that makes him a de-Capulet. Did he bite his thumb
at him? He did, but not directly, for that is against the
law. He bit his thumb simply. The Prince will have
them both fried in oil before Tuesday a week.

[*They go off chattering.*]

JULIET [*looking after them*]:
  Infamous fellow, yellow-livered lout!
  'Tis not the Prince who has us on the spit,
  But vanished youth and wedded circumstance.
  Man is an island nibbled by the sea,
  On which he nurtures weeds to hold the soil,
  And sometimes in his youth and by the moon,
  Names one a flower and calls the preacher in.
  April was full of birds and meadow-things;
  We had no May; we came too fast to June.
  And now—July? And there's no blossom left;
  No bud or bush to tempt the butterfly
  Or plundering bee to dredge the honey up.
  And if there were—what honey is there left?
  No, Juliet! No! A woman's not a weed,
  Nor yet a bush. A woman is a wasp!
  And has a sting to cure tarantulas
  Caught in the bushes with a dragonfly!
  So let me use it. I shall place it so.
  Since constancy is taken for a fool,
  Virtue for madness, innocence for fraud,
  I'll take what comes, put modesty to school,
  And learn from Romeo to be a bawd!
  I'll play his game and rob him of his bite.
  If one can kiss, then two can kiss tonight!

[*A* TIPSY MAN *has been making his way toward her across the Square. He comes to her.*]

MAN: Good evening, sweetheart! How about a little
  ki . . . ?

[*He tries to put his arm around her. She rises in sudden fury, and hits him with the feather boa; it wraps itself around his face, and he staggers off in confusion.* JULIET

89

*looks after him, then puts her face down in her hands.
After a moment, she walks off slowly in the opposite
direction. A* CHILD'S VOICE *is heard singing*]:
> Lavender's blue, dilly dilly,
> Lavender's green
> When I am king, dilly dilly,
> You shall be Queen.

CURTAIN

SCENE II

[*A room in the Montague Palace, late night.* FRIAR
LAURENCE *is seated comfortably on a chair L., talking—
and listening—to* ROMEO *who is stretched out on a couch
in front of him; it is the classic position of the analyst.
Upstage R., a table with powders in vials, mortar and
pestle.*]

FRIAR LAURENCE: You say she left the forest, and was
    gone? And that you haven't seen her? By my holy
    order, I thought your disposition better tempered!
    Whatever got into you, anyway? Brawling and duel-
    ing . . . at your age! Like a peevish schoolboy—
ROMEO: I'm very unhappy.
FRIAR LAURENCE: And so are most men. Yet you of all
    men, I should think, would have least to cry about.
ROMEO: I cry for Juliet.

FRIAR LAURENCE: Then save your tears for yourself. The girl only put up with you all these years because of her sweet nature.

ROMEO: It's really for myself I cry, Father. For being so much less than what I am . . . or am I? There's the rub. What good opinion have I left of me? I liked myself when I was young. I was on fire then, and had no doubt about it.

FRIAR LAURENCE: All youth's like that. Fire, or ice—or sometimes both together.

ROMEO: Then youth should never marry, but die young.

[JULIET *comes in at the door upper R., unseen by the others; she hears their voices, and stands still, listening. She looks tired, and rumpled.*]

FRIAR LAURENCE [*Sees her, but* ROMEO *does not.* FRIAR LAURENCE *makes no sign*]:   Then who would marry, boy? Or was your father never young?

ROMEO: My father young? . . . [*Surprised*] Why—I suppose he was. You know—it never occurred to me. Or my mother, either. You mean. . . ? No! That's incredible! I'll not believe it!

FRIAR LAURENCE: Believe what you like. You're here; and you were born—

ROMEO: Faugh! . . . Leastways, my mother never left my father standing like a ninny in the woods, bawling her name.

FRIAR LAURENCE: And what does that mean to you, my son?

ROMEO [*rising, goes to table, reaches for powder in mortar*]:   Nothing. I dream of dragons and manticores. Tell me why, Father.

FRIAR LAURENCE [*rising, following him*]:   You tell me why, my son . . . That's not ready yet.

[*Takes powder from him and grinds it.*]

ROMEO: I tried to find her. Do you think she's really left me? For good?

FRIAR LAURENCE: I doubt it very much. She has too many years invested in you.

ROMEO: It was such a small thing—as it was meant. No more than a moment. Caught in the bushes like a fox with a pullet!

FRIAR LAURENCE: Is that what troubles you—that you were caught?

ROMEO: No. I wanted to be Juliet's lover—not a clown.

FRIAR LAURENCE [*sits*]:   Ah!

[JULIET'S *face is gentled.*]

ROMEO: It was my longing to be young again. I went too lightly; and I went astray. I never meant it, Father.

FRIAR LAURENCE: Did you enjoy it?

ROMEO [*turning downstage—honestly*]:   I did. At the moment.

[JULIET *looks stormy.*]

FRIAR LAURENCE: I suppose this is some sort of confession . . .

ROMEO [*returns and kneels beside table*]:   Then shrive me, Father; confess me, and give me absolution. I may need it tomorrow.

FRIAR LAURENCE: I cannot shrive you. But it will do you good to talk.

ROMEO: It's not that I mind dying. But I have wounded Juliet; and that spoils the story. For I love her, Father, and no other—and so in a way I've driven the dagger into my own heart—or else taken poison; and this time from no cheating apothecary, but myself. [*He starts down R.*] Romeo and Juliet . . . young girls and boys would have told each other our story, they would have whispered our names between their kisses. What a failure I've made of it, Father—in what I wanted to do best; to love one woman through eternity!

[JULIET *starts forward joyously, but* FRIAR LAURENCE *rises and makes a sign for her to be quiet; he comes down R., holding a powder and a glass.*]

FRIAR LAURENCE: And will you love her best by getting yourself killed tomorrow morning?

ROMEO [*continuing his own thought*]:   . . . And to live happily ever after. [*Rousing himself to answer* FRIAR LAURENCE] Too late to think of that.

FRIAR LAURENCE [*giving the glass and the powder to* ROMEO]:   You've had many quarrels, my son—you and Juliet; and this, maybe, the worst of any. But aren't they always the same? "Do you love me?" they say: "do you really love me?"

[*Unseen by* ROMEO, *he looks quickly and meaningfully toward* JULIET.]

ROMEO: It's true. I cannot bear not to be loved.

FRIAR LAURENCE [*returning to the table*]:   Nor she, either. The two of you cannot bear it, and must needs be told every day—It's that you're always asking each other in the midst of blows—"Do you love me?"!

[*He turns toward* JULIET.]

[JULIET *smiles and blows a kiss to* FRIAR LAURENCE, *who makes a little gesture of benediction. She turns and tiptoes off.*]

FRIAR LAURENCE [*briskly*]:   Suppose you kill this Paris? You'll be hanged for it—and all my pains for nothing.

[*coming down R. with a glass of water, which he gives* Romeo] And if you wound him? What then? More years in foreign parts?

romeo [*crossing to L., mixing the potion; bitterly*]:   I might be better off among strangers, than here at home.

[*He drinks and grimaces.*]

friar laurence [*sighing*]:   Ah well . . . if that's the way it is, and if there's no way to stop this sinful duel — My son, you've said a lot of things to me were far better said to your wife. Go say them to her. [Romeo *stands, despondent, his back turned to* Friar Laurence. *At this point* Friar Laurence *turns him gently around.* Romeo *is at first unbelieving, then he lights up.* Friar Laurence *escorts him toward upper L., their backs to the audience.*]   Something tells me she's come home again. May God forgive me for saying it—[*He crosses himself*]—but you would do better to commend yourself to *her* grace, than to *His!*

[Romeo *rushes out.* Friar Laurence, *alone*]

Friar Laurence [*sadly*]:   Or to mine.

[Romeo *dashes back, gives the glass to* Friar Laurence.]

romeo: Thank you, Father.

friar laurence [*coming downstage*]:   I have blundered too much already in this affair; I should have listened to caution and the law, instead of to my heart. That sleeping draught I gave to Juliet . . . that brought it all about . . . And now more blood; and after that more tears, either for Juliet or Rosaline. Mea culpa, Domine, mea culpa! Our Saint rejoiced in marriages of birds; he knew that marriages of men were better made in

94

heaven! [*He sighs; then, struck by a sudden horrid thought*] . . . Heaven forbid it! Ten more years of Mantua—?

[*He sees the glass in his hand, and hastily drinks what is left of the potion.*]

CURTAIN

SCENE III

ROSALINE's *boudoir in the Paris household.* ROSALINE *is found in negligee, seated at her escritoire, writing a letter. She finishes it, reads it over to herself, signs it, pours sand over it, seals it, and pulls the bell-pull for a* SERVANT *who immediately appears, and to whom she hands the letter.*

ROSALINE: Take this to Lady Capu—I mean Montague.
SERVANT: Will there be an answer, my Lady?
ROSALINE [*almost to herself*]:   Who knows . . .? [*to the* SERVANT]: There may not be an answer . . .
SERVANT: Yes, my Lady.
[*He takes the letter and exits.* ROSALINE *seats herself at her dressing table, and starts to brush her hair.*]
ROSALINE [*musing*]:

How small a thing to hold so wide a woe!
A child, a girl, a woman, and a wife,

All in a space no larger than my heart!
The braided infant greedy for her sweets,
Then the young maiden wedded to the moon,
In love with virtue and the minuet—
Turned to a wife too soon.

                              An early wife,
Wearing her husband like a featherbed.
And then the mother with her buttery brood . . .
What! Shall I now be widowed in the world
Before my morning chocolate?

                              For what good?
It was an artless, uncorrupted kiss,
That was but given to a frightened girl
Who saw some silver in a school friend's hair.
I'll not be made a mourner out of that!
The shrew has teeth for all her gentle fare.
I've done the best I could.

                              The rest, I think,
Is Juliet's . . .

[PARIS *enters in his nightshirt*]

PARIS: Look here, Rosaline.

ROSALINE: Don't touch me!

PARIS [*sinking down again*]:   Damme—I protest! You'd
think *I* was the guilty one!

ROSALINE: And weren't you? You and that Capulet
woman! What were *you* doing in the bushes, pray?

PARIS [*stuttering with indignation*]:   What was I doing?
Why—why—nothing, of course! But *you*—!

ROSALINE [*coldly*]:   Romeo is an old old friend. I was
never engaged to him—as you were, to Juliet.

PARIS: We weren't engaged. Not officially. We were

never more than circumspectly met; and always with the nurse.

ROSALINE: That looked the other way now and then for convenience' sake?

PARIS: Rosaline—this is not like you. You are not yourself.

ROSALINE: But I am. Paris—for the once! For a moment —one moment—I was young again. Until you came crashing through the bushes!

PARIS: Rosaline—I don't understand you. How can you—

ROSALINE [*interrupting*]: What have I had these ten long years? Four children, evenly spaced; the season in Verona, the season in Viareggio.

PARIS: Can I help it if Joseph has the croup?

ROSALINE [*rushing on*]: Yes, Madam to the Duchess, No, Madam to the Princess, Yes, Madam here, No Madam there—and no help with the dining room chairs! What sort of a life is that?

PARIS: I do protest, Rosaline—

ROSALINE: And what's more—please explain to me what you meant by having Romeo apologize to Juliet? Whose husband are you anyway?

PARIS [*floundering*]: Why—I—it seemed to me—I mean to say—

ROSALINE [*calm*]: Are you going to challenge him?

PARIS: Of course. Can't help myself.

ROSALINE: Remember what he did to you the last time. He'd have skewered you like a rabbit, except his foot slipped or something.

PARIS [*uncomfortably*]: Oh—well—my timing was a bit off—

ROSALINE: You're older now, Paris. Your timing's older now, too.

PARIS: So is his.

ROSALINE: I wouldn't be too sure.

PARIS: Hm. Hm. Well—what am I to do, Rosaline? After all, my honor—

ROSALINE: You're to choose pistols. That's what you're to do.

PARIS: Pistols? I protest—that's devilish dangerous!

ROSALINE: And what about swords? All points and sharp edges . . . No one ever yet fought but got himself cut with them. Lunge here, lunge there, hui hui . . . trip over a tree root, and end up with two inches of steel either in yourself, or Romeo . . .

PARIS [*bravely*]: Ha!

ROSALINE: Give over, Paris! Remember the last time.

PARIS: Damme, Roz—you keep throwing it up to me! I tell you, it was accidental . . .

ROSALINE: And so would this be! You haven't put your mind to it at all.

PARIS: Suppose . . . he shoots me!

ROSALINE: Let *me* attend to that.

PARIS: Really, my dear—! He might at that, you know.

ROSALINE: And have Juliet spend ten more years in Mantua?

PARIS: By Jove—! Rosaline—you *are* an intelligent creature!

ROSALINE: Thank you. And you know something else, Paris? I'm rather attractive, too—I'm told.

PARIS: Why—yes you are, you know; no doubt about it. Ah—er—well, let's to bed—?

ROSALINE: As you wish, my dear. [*She rises, and starts to blow out the candles*] So evenly spaced . . .

CURTAIN

SCENE IV

The Montague Palace. JULIET's *bath.* JULIET *is in the tub, a large sunken Romanesque affair; and the* NURSE *is washing her back.*

JULIET, *in the tub, looks up at the* NURSE.

JULIET [*thoughtfully*]:   I don't think I *want* to stop it, Nurse.

NURSE: It's a sin, that's what it is. A mortal sin. A duel is a mortal sin, no matter who's dead afterwards.

JULIET: I'm not sure I know what sin is. Is it a sin to be happy? [*She rises from the tub—modestly screened by the* NURSE, *who wraps her at once in a large towel.*] I am expectant, Nurse. Nine months from tonight—

NURSE: Holy Saint Peter!—or else Saint Joseph . . . And your husband may be killed in the morning! [JULIET *goes to her dressing table; the* NURSE—*always hiding her from the audience—puts her dressing gown around her.* JULIET *brushes her hair.*]

JULIET: He won't be killed. Paris is a dreadfully poor shot.

99

NURSE: And what if Romeo kills him?—as he did Tybalt.

JULIET: They fought with swords. Someone was bound to be hurt.

NURSE: He won't get out of it so lightly this time!

JULIET [*gravely*]:   No one gets lightly out of anything. No one goes lightly out of life . . . or comes lightly into it. I know he loves me, Nurse dear. It's worth a scratch——isn't it? I'd take the wound myself, and happily!

NURSE: Not now you wouldn't, child. And you with a new Capulet in your belly—or is it a Montague—? [*She stops, obviously puzzled.*] . . . Nine months . . . from *tonight?*

JULIET [*mischievously*]:   How do I look, Nurse? Like a mooning girl?

NURSE: Aye! That you do!

JULIET [*gaily*]:   A little more berry juice on my cheeks? Those tallow cheeks, Nurse?

NURSE: La!

JULIET: And scent! . . . Heliotrope? or jasmine?

NURSE: A drop . . .

JULIET: Oh . . . ! All over! I shall be drenched in moonlight!

NURSE: Glory be! [*She gathers up the towels and bath things, and starts out into the bedroom.*] I'll have something of my own again! To spank his little bottom and feed him peppermint! He'll be a flower. A very flower! Nine months—from *tonight. . ? !*

[NURSE *goes out.*]

JULIET [*alone*]:

A mooning girl . . . and fortune on a throw! . . .
Not gold or silver, but a nothing thing,
A dream, a cry, a longing, a man's need

To see himself less faithless than he is.
No man's a monster wholly—or he's mad;
But mad men even sing from time to time
And draw some beauty upward from the heart
Like waters to the moon. What if he dreams
Of nobler panoramas of the soul,
Than what he shows us? How reduced they are
Who'd turn our eyes in blinders from that hope,
And show a man as so much wormy meal
Stuck for a moment on a speck of dust
Halfway from here to nowhere! So they say.
What matters if our hearts grow faint and die
Of malnutrition? Why, it matters this:
That joy and grief, which are love's ministers,
Furnish the heart more sweetly than those thoughts
Which profit only on our wretchedness.
So then—to arms! If nature does design
That two and two make four for Rosaline,
Why then, I'll prove that one and one make two,
Or heart ne'er told a woman what to do!

SCENE V

The bedroom, candlelight. ROMEO *enters the bedroom.
He stands a moment, looking toward the bathroom; to*
JULIET *in the doorway. She is smiling a little. She looks
gentle and lovely.*

ROMEO: Julie . . . Have I acted very badly?

JULIET: Yes, darling . . . I'm afraid so.

ROMEO: We should never have come back here. You said that once . . . remember?

JULIET: I meant it differently, I think.

ROMEO: It's our families, Julie. They set us at each other.

JULIET [*serenely*]:   They may as well give over, then; I'll never be a proper Montague. Or you a Capulet.

ROMEO: I know what Mercutio meant. A plague on both our houses!

JULIET: He was only a boy . . . and Tybalt, too. So young! . . . [*She turns to him with a sudden rise of anxiety.*] Romeo! Tomorrow morning . . ? Darling . . .

ROMEO: You know, then? He's chosen pistols.

JULIET: I had a note from Rosaline.

ROMEO: I see. Then I'm forgiven there. [*He pauses and sighs.*] Julie—

JULIET: Yes, darling?

ROMEO: I wish I could believe in love, and in myself again!

JULIET: And not in me?

ROMEO: I cannot think of love without naming you.

JULIET: Name me, then! I'm glad it happened. Because there's only one thing we need to know: that spring is only a little season between bud and blossoming. But summer is a long time. A long, long time, my dear.

ROMEO: And shall we live happily in summer, Julie?

JULIET: Yes . . . No . . . Not *all* the time. Only children live happily ever after. But at least . . .

ROMEO: Yes, love?

JULIET: We'll keep each other company!

[*They embrace.* Romeo *extinguishes the candles. In the
gentle darkness, a* Child's Voice *is heard singing*]:

Lavender's blue, dilly dilly,
Lavender's green . . .

CURTAIN

SCENE VI

The Square in Verona
[Prince Escalus *comes on, followed by* Courtiers]
ESCALUS:

The fires we thought were dead have sprung to life.
Contagion reigns, and swords are in the street.
Lord Paris and the stormy Montague
Darken our peace. I will not have this strife!
If either one shall run the other through,
I'll have him out of here before his youth
Has chance to rise to bid his wife adieu.
The Night is on us. Herald, sound retreat.
God gave us wisdom and the strength to rule;
Princes are known to have died from too much sweet.
We are too easy on the ill-disposed,
And favor those who from their angry blood
Make others suffer for their melancholy.
Wherefrom the very stars must turn away,
Having a horror of such circumstance—
Or else, a mirror of our bloody times,

103

Oppose our field and show us to ourselves
In reverse order, which, if we do meet
Head on, like two great monsters in a wood,
We do destroy ourselves—or so they say.
They even tell us that the earth is curved
And that the sun is steadfast in the sky
And we go round. I'm no philosopher,
But this I know: if man's to stay his course
Upon this ball of roses and of stones,
He must find ways to settle arguments
That do not fill the earth with broken bones,
Insult the innocent with unjust force,
Or make this land a private park of war.
So then, good friends, to bed. The day is o'er;
It is long past the falling of the dew.
The Land is still, the city quiet too.
Proud Montague! Rebellious Capulet!
We'll sheathe the daggers of your passions yet!

[*As the* PRINCE *starts to leave the stage, the* PAPARAZZI
come forward to interview him.]

PAPARAZZI NO. 1:

Sir—in regard to the war with Mantua . . .

PRINCE:

The war? What war?
There is no war with Mantua. By the Rood,
There is but disagreement! For the Guelph,
Faced by imperial-minded Ghibelline,
Cries out for freedom and election's voice!
Our brother Pope himself is in the fight,
And battles Satan for the souls of men,
Bidding them dream of freedom's holy light
And choose the manner of their servitude.

PAPARAZZI NO. 2:

And if the vote's against our side—what then?

PRINCE:

We shall demand that Mantua vote again!

[*There is a general murmur.*]

Our joys, our griefs, our manners and our laws,
Deserve respect, attention, and applause.
Let all men know that as we choose to live,
So shall they too—or else a forfeit give!
And as I am the Prince of this dear city,
My word is absolute.

PAPARAZZI NO. 1:

And more's the pity!

[*They all follow the* PRINCE *off.*]

CURTAIN

S C E N E   V I I

A meadow at dawn.

ROMEO *and his party arrive, muffled in long cloaks and wearing dominoes. The party consists of* ROMEO, JULIET, *the* NURSE, *and* FRIAR LAURENCE. *They stand in silence for a moment.*

ROMEO [*to* FRIAR LAURENCE]:   Let me see the pistols.

[FRIAR LAURENCE *holds out a box of duelling pistols;*

ROMEO *takes one, balances it, and aims at a tree.*]   It will do well enough.

NURSE: Be careful, Master Romeo! That thing could go off!

FRIAR LAURENCE [*drawing his robe around him*]:   I had more comfort in my little cell.

ROMEO: I say, Julie—did you bring the eggs and the sausages?

JULIET: Here they are.

[*She brings forth a basket from under her cloak.*]

NURSE: Look—I brought a pot of chocolate—

ROMEO: Good!

FRIAR LAURENCE: Splendid! For a cold morning . . . nothing like hot chocolate. . . .

JULIET: We may as well be comfortable—

ROMEO: Quite. Morning's at the rise. I hear the lark.

JULIET: Are you sure? I think it is the . . .

ROMEO: It is the lark. Or County Paris whistling in the dark.

[*Enter* PARIS, ROSALINE, *and* LORD *and* LADY CAPULET.]

PARIS: I see you have arrived before me. I thought to bring my witnesses, in case—

LADY CAPULET: Good morning, Romeo.

ROMEO: Good morrow, Mother.

LORD CAPULET [*coolly*]:   Juliet—

JULIET: Father—

LADY CAPULET [*to* JULIET]:   We have some pickled herring and a cold bird . . . for light refreshment . . .

ROMEO: Later, Ma'am. Paris and I have some prior business with each other.

[*He motions to* FRIAR LAURENCE, *who comes forward and offers the box of pistols to* LORD CAPULET, *who ex-*

amines it, nods, and hands it on to PARIS. PARIS *takes a pistol.*]

PARIS: This is too heavy. Let me see another. [*He takes up the other one.*]   This likes me well. I have been in continual practice since I went to France. I shall win at the odds.

FRIAR LAURENCE [*to* ROMEO]:   That's from *Hamlet*, boy.

ROMEO: Well, so it is, but let be; the man is educated. Let's hope he's learned to miss the mark! Otherwise . . . ! Well—shall we commence?

FRIAR LAURENCE: I shall begin the count-down. While you two gentlemen walk each to his own side, and at the point of five you shall each one turn and fire, at will, or with immediate aim. . . . Is it understood?

ROMEO & PARIS: Understood.

[ROMEO *and* PARIS *stand back to back, holding their pistols at the ready.* FRIAR LAURENCE *starts to count.*]

FRIAR LAURENCE: One, Two, Three, Four . . .

[*Before* FRIAR LAURENCE *has finished counting,* JULIET *and* ROSALINE *walk up to their husbands and take the pistols from their hands.*]

JULIET: Now, Rosaline!

ROSALINE: Now, Juliet!

[ROMEO *and* PARIS *fall back in surprise.* JULIET *and* ROSALINE *keep the pistols trained on them.*]

ROMEO: Juliet! What the devil—?

JULIET: Stand back, my love—

PARIS: Rosaline—I say!—

ROSALINE: Don't move, my dear. This pistol might go off—

CAPULET: Juliet—I forbid this!

LADY CAPULET: My God!

JULIET [*waving the pistol at her* FATHER]:   Stand back, Father! Romeo—hold him up; he's going to faint.

CAPULET [*clutching at* ROMEO]:   My boy . . . my boy . . .

ROMEO: Trust her, sir. She's a solid girl.

FRIAR LAURENCE [*stepping forward*]:   Ladies. . . !

JULIET: Be quiet, Father. Having brought it all about in the first place, it's only right that we ladies attend to this ourselves. [*To* ROSALINE] When I count five?

ROSALINE: When you count five. [*To* PARIS] Don't forget to take the children to their grandmother on Sunday—

PARIS [*to* ROMEO]:   Good God! They're in earnest! Do something!

ROMEO [*aghast*]:   They *can't* be! It's against nature!

ROSALINE: Come, Juliet. The count!

JULIET: Excuse me. One, two, three, four . . . [*to* ROMEO] Give my feather boa to my mother. Five—

[*The* TWO WOMEN *close their eyes tightly and fire in the general direction of the air.* ROMEO *and* PARIS *cover their eyes;* LADY CAPULET *falls into* NURSE's *arms, who fans her.* CAPULET *sinks to the ground.*]

CAPULET: Oh . . . I'm too old for this sort of thing! Juliet . . . !

[ROMEO *and* PARIS *rush to embrace their wives.*]

ROMEO: Darling! You had me frightened for a moment—

JULIET [*weakly*]:   Only a moment?

[*They embrace.*]

PARIS: A heroine, by God!

ROSALINE: It was nothing. [*Her knees buckle.*]

ROMEO [*to* PARIS, *noticing* ROSALINE's *distress*]:   Oh—I say—

PARIS: Give me a hand, old boy, will you?

ROMEO: Gladly—

[*Together they deposit* ROSALINE *on a convenient hassock.*]

LADY CAPULET: I was never so frightened in my life!

JULIET: Now, Mother—you saw me dead once before.

NURSE: It's like old times, my Lady!

PARIS: Rosaline! Rest!

ROSALINE: Yes, dear—

PARIS [*to the others; awkwardly*]: I mean to say . . . last night, you know . . .

JULIET [*to* ROSALINE]: You too?

ROSALINE [*with a not-too-rueful sigh*]: Probably.

JULIET [*She embraces* ROSALINE]: My dear! Here's a kiss for number five. And one for Joseph, croup and all! Oh—I hope mine is a boy!

ROSALINE: I hope so, too.

CAPULET: What's this? What's this? This puts a new light on things. A boy, eh? Hmm! Your hand, Romeo. You've made your point. A solid throw!

ROMEO: Why, thank you, sir. I'm sure he'll be an honor to the . . . Capulets.

CAPULET: Thank you, my boy. Thank you, son. That's very kind of you. Very kind, I'm sure.

ROMEO: Well—I shall be off . . .

JULIET [*surprised*]: Where to, my love?

ROMEO: Why—to make my fortune in the city.

CAPULET: Eh? What's this?

PARIS: By George! I say—Romeo—I need a manager for my herring factory—

ROMEO: No, my friend. I would have thanked you

once—but I've been a herring too long. I've been promised employment by the Prince, in a position proper to a man of substance, the father of a Montague *and* a Capulet.

CAPULET: And I shall make over to my grandson my winery in Asti. [*Fondly, to* JULIET] Tallow face!

JULIET [*laughing, embracing him*]:   Father!

LADY CAPULET: Oh—good, Cappy!

[LORD *and* LADY MONTAGUE *enter rapidly, and out of breath.*]

LORD MONTAGUE: I forbid it! This duel must cease! I have here a writ of replevin, or whatever . . . signed by our gracious Prince. . . .

ROMEO: Give over, Father. All's well that ends well! Our shots are fired, honor satisfied, and no one the worse.

LADY MONTAGUE: What a relief! It's so much better to quarrel peaceably, in the family.

LADY CAPULET: Come, Montagues. We have a table spread.

LORD MONTAGUE: Why, thank you, Ma'am. I confess, I'm hungry. Somebody took my breakfast sausage from the house—

NURSE: A cold bird . . . eggs . . . hot chocolate . . . herring . . . sausages . . .

LORD MONTAGUE: Sausages!

FRIAR LAURENCE: Now Paris—Rosaline . . . do you join us?

ROSALINE: Indeed we do, and in all happiness . . .

[*All arrange themselves around the cloth except* ROMEO *and* JULIET, *who come forward.*]

JULIET:

> So ends our story where it was begun;
> The night has dimmed its candles one by one.

ROMEO:

> Forgive us if we've chronicled askew
> This tale of Capulet and Montague—
> Thus fancying—since grief did not prevail—

JULIET: 'Twas all a lark!

ROMEO: —and not a nightingale!

CURTAIN

BOOKS BY

ROBERT NATHAN

Novels

THE MALLOT DIARIES (*1965*)

THE FAIR (*1964*)

THE DEVIL WITH LOVE (*1963*)

A STAR IN THE WIND (*1962*)

THE WILDERNESS-STONE (*1961*)

THE COLOR OF EVENING (*1960*)

SO LOVE RETURNS (*1958*)

THE RANCHO OF THE LITTLE LOVES (*1956*)

SIR HENRY (*1955*)   THE TRAIN IN THE MEADOW (*1953*)

THE INNOCENT EVE (*1951*)   THE MARRIED LOOK (*1950*)

THE ADVENTURES OF TAPIOLA (*1950*)

(*containing* JOURNEY OF TAIPOLA, *1938,*

and TAPIOLA'S BRAVE REGIMENT, *1941*)

THE RIVER JOURNEY (*1949*)

LONG AFTER SUMMER (*1948*)

MR. WHITTLE AND THE MORNING STAR (*1947*)

BUT GENTLY DAY (*1943*)   THE SEA-GULL CRY (*1942*)

THEY WENT ON TOGETHER (*1941*)

PORTRAIT OF JENNIE (*1940*)   WINTER IN APRIL (*1938*)

THE BARLY FIELDS (*1938*)

(*containing* THE FIDDLER IN BARLY, *1926,*

THE WOODCUTTER'S HOUSE, *1927,*

THE BISHOP'S WIFE, *1928,* THE ORCHID, *1931,*

and THERE IS ANOTHER HEAVEN, *1929*)

THE ENCHANTED VOYAGE (*1936*)   ROAD OF AGES (*1935*)

ONE MORE SPRING (*1933*)   JONAH (*1925*)

Poems

THE MARRIED MAN (*1962*)   THE GREEN LEAF (*1950*)
THE DARKENING MEADOWS (*1945*)
MORNING IN IOWA (*1944*)   DUNKIRK (*1941*)
A WINTER TIDE (*1940*)   SELECTED POEMS (*1935*)

Theater

JEZEBEL'S HUSBAND & THE SLEEPING BEAUTY (*1953*)

For Young People

THE SNOWFLAKE AND THE STARFISH (*1959*)

Archaeology

THE WEANS (*1960*)

These are BORZOI BOOKS, *published in New York*
by ALFRED A. KNOPF

A NOTE ABOUT THE AUTHOR

ROBERT NATHAN was born in New York City in 1894 and was educated at private schools in the United States and Switzerland. While attending Harvard University he was an editor of the *Harvard Monthly,* in which his first stories and poems appeared. Except for two short periods during which he was a solicitor for a New York advertising firm and a teacher in the School of Journalism of New York University, Mr. Nathan has devoted his time exclusively to writing. He is the author of over forty volumes of poetry and prose, and from this body of distinguished work he has acquired a reputation as a master of satiric fantasy unique in American letters. He lives now in California with his wife, who was Miss Helen Shirley Kneeland, of Salem, Massachusetts.

A NOTE ON THE TYPE

The text of this book is set in Caledonia, a Lino-type face designed by W. A. Dwiggins (1880–1956), the man who was responsible for so much that is good in contemporary book design and typography. Caledonia belongs to the family of printing types called "modern face" by printers— a term used to mark the change in style of type-letters that occurred about 1800. Caledonia borders on the general design of Scotch Modern but is more freely drawn than that letter.

The book was composed, printed, and bound by The Book Press Incorporated, Brattleboro, Ver-mont.

Typography by Jaime Davidovich